Hidden Wealth

Unlocking the wealth within

Elizabeth Benjamin

© Copyright 2018 Elizabeth Benjamin

The right of Elizabeth Benjamin to be identified as the Author of the work has been asserted in accordance with the Copyright, Designs and Patent Act 1988.
All rights reserved. No part of this publication may be reproduced, stored in a retrieval system or transmitted, in any form or by any means, without the prior written permission of the author, be otherwise circulated in any form of binding or cover, other than that in which it is published. A CIP catalogue record for this title is available from the British Library.
ISBN: 978-1-64606-827-2
Book cover design and layout by: www.wearereach.org
Printed by: www.wearereach.org

Unless otherwise noted all Scripture is taken from the King James Version of the Holy Bible.
The Authorised (King James) Version of the Bible ('the KJV'), the rights in which are vested in the Crown in the United Kingdom, is reproduced here by permission of the Crown's patentee, Cambridge University Press.
The Cambridge KJV text including paragraphing, is reproduced here by permission of Cambridge University Press.
Scriptures taken from The Holy Bible, New International Version®, NIV® Copyright © 1973, 1978, 1984, 2011 by Biblica, Inc.® Used by permission. All rights reserved worldwide.
Scripture quotations are taken from the HOLY BIBLE, New Living Translation, copyright © 1996, 2004, 2015 by Tyndale House Foundation. Used by permission of Tyndale House Publishers, Inc., Carol Stream, Illinois 60188. All rights reserved.
Scriptures taken from The ESV® Bible (The Holy Bible, English Standard Version®). ESV® Text Edition: 2016. Copyright © 2001 by Crossway, a publishing ministry of Good News Publishers.
Scripture taken from the New King James Version®. Copyright © 1982 by Thomas Nelson. Used by permission. All rights reserved.

APPRECIATION

I would like to express my appreciation and gratitude to the men and women who have inspired me and helped me along my personal journey of wealth creation:

- *Mr Graham and Mrs Daphne Rowan of Elite Investors United Kingdom*

- *Mr Elias Saad a Goodwill Ambassador of Maldives and Chairman and CEO of RATCON CONSTRUCTION and Eko Pearl Lagos, Nigeria*

- *Dr Mike Murdock, Senior Pastor of The Wisdom Centre USA*

- *Dr Bill Winston, founder of Living Word Christian Centre USA*

- *Pastor Matthew Ashimolowo, Senior Pastor of Kingsway International Christian Centre United Kingdom*

- *Mr Otabil of International Central Gospel Church Ghana*

Your priceless passion, wisdom, energy and mentorship have been of tremendous value to me.

Table of Contents

Introduction	1
Chapter One: BELIEVE	9
Chapter Two: MIND MATTERS	21
Chapter Three: ATTITUDE	33
Chapter Four: HABIT	43
Chapter Five: ACTION	53
Chapter Six: PILLARS OF WEALTH CREATION	79
Chapter Seven: THE WORD IN ACTION	107
Conclusion	121

INTRODUCTION

This book is designed as a self-help guide detailing how the application of certain key principles will unlock your hidden wealth. Through it, I aim to help you learn how to rule your finances by unlocking the prosperity and blessing that has already been made available, so you can take financial dominion once and for all!

Go Deeper

Precious stones and metals like gold and diamonds, which are of great value, are not found on the surface.

In the Bible from the book of Luke we see that Jesus gave Simon, a fisherman by trade, a clear instruction:

*Now when he had left speaking, he said unto Simon, 'Launch out into the **deep**, and let down your nets for a draught.' – Luke 5:4*

Until Simon followed this instruction and launched into the **deep**, he and the other fishermen with him were just toiling. WORKING HARDER WILL NOT NECESSARILY CREATE WEALTH. It is using the potential, hidden inside you, that will launch you into your wealthy place.

Again, Jesus taught in a parable about laying a good foundation when building a house. One man built on a solid foundation of rock – the roots would have been dug deep into the ground to cause it to withstand the storm. If you can dig deep then your 'roots' and foundation will be strong enough to sustain continual increase and wealth creation.

Remember although each individual has been given unique potential, we all have two main common resources everyone has been given to create wealth: TIME and OPPORTUNITY which are common to all men. Opportunity is revealed in the **problems around YOU. Recognise that YOU have hidden ability** (potential) to solve the problems around you. Your potential is unique to you and it will enable you to solve specific problems no one else can solve; that is where your wealth is! So, it does not matter if you are in a vocational role or profession – nor does it matter whether you are from the first or third world; time and opportunity are available to you!

DEVELOP YOUR MAIN GIFT AND YOUR OTHER GIFTS, AS POTENTIAL NEVER RUNS OUT. The Bible says in Proverbs 18:16 that a man's gift makes room for him and brings him before great people. As you can see, it's **YOUR GIFT that will MAKE ROOM for you AND BRING YOU BEFORE GREAT MEN; in other words, establish who you are. But it is how you then develop the gifts and produce more gifts, i.e. multiply them into extra gifts, that will create wealth.**

Michael Jordan, Usain Bolt and Serena Williams are all excellent examples of this. They each honed their gifts and multiplied their talents to become some of the greatest athletes in the world. Yes, their main gifting might be in sport, which shot them to stardom, but it's how they developed their gifting and other talents that sustained them, after their sporting career, and allowed them to build their wealth. Even once retired, the promotional deals and royalties they build up in advertising and other areas will continue to create their wealth.

Hidden Wealth

Mike Tyson's main gift as a boxer made room for him but his other gifts were not developed, and he squandered about $300m. In 2013 Tyson filed for bankruptcy. On the other hand, Michael Jackson whose main gift was singing and song writing, allowed his gifts to make room for him. But, his estate, investments and other areas of promotional deals established him even when he had passed on. His investments in film and TV rights, including his purchase of publishing rights to the Beetles song catalogue for $47.5m,[i] all yielded him great profit. An interesting article from gobankingrates.com on the net worth of celebrities who have died said the following:

"Michael Jackson's estate had made over $1b. When Michael Jackson died in 2009, the estate belonging to the 50-year-old singer was bankrupt. In the years that followed, however, the estate became a lucrative property, generating billions off album sales, the film 'Michael Jackson's This Is It' and the Cirque du Soleil show 'Michael Jackson: One.'"

In 2016, Michael Jackson's estate made another $750 million when it sold its remaining stake in a music catalogue to Sony. The deal gave Sony sole ownership of works recorded by The Beatles, Bob Dylan and other best-selling artists. In 2017, Jackson topped Forbes' list of top-earning dead celebrities for the fifth year in a row, with $75 million in earnings for the year.'

Most people say they are poor because they are made that way and they don't have control over their situation. This mentality is wrong!

The main cause of poverty is rooted in *belief systems*. The issue is, people don't believe in who they are, what they have and what they need to do with what they have. You

may say, 'But I don't have anything.' Well, everything that is visible comes from the invisible realm – including you! You were on the mind of your Creator even before your father and mother brought you into the world and met you. Everything you see began with a thought, an idea, and was created – made to appear – by things you cannot see. So, what does this mean for you and your hidden wealth? The answer is simple: <u>*You have hidden potential that you can turn into abundance.*</u>

When you were created, you were given the potential to create things and make this world a better place. Do you know how much authority you have available to you? It may not seem or feel like you have any authority at times, but that doesn't change how God designed you. From the beginning, **dominion** was His plan for you, He gave you dominion over the earth and *everything* in it as we see in <u>Genesis 1:28</u> which says, 'And God blessed them, and God said unto them, Be fruitful, and multiply, and replenish the earth, and subdue it: and have dominion over the fish of the sea, and over the fowl of the air, and over every living thing that moveth upon the earth.' Although Satan stole this position – God made a way through Jesus' victory on the cross. Authority was returned to mankind so that you are free to stand in your rightful position, ensuring your dominion and authority over sickness, disease and strife, as well as POVERTY, LACK and anything else under the curse.

We are not created to sweat and labour incessantly for our provision. Yes, we should work but it's a different kind of work. When you first start out and begin work, *you should work to bring out your potential*, hidden inside you, and wherever you find yourself at this moment in time you should be moving towards a bigger goal that doesn't limit you or trap you on the 9-5 treadmill because your potential is limitless!

When it comes to money, do you feel like you have financial dominion and authority over your finances? Or do bills, debt and work-related troubles seem to rule *you* instead? The world, the media and everyone around you seems to be under the weight of constant financial pressure – even worse, they make you feel as though you should be too.

Consider this question: **Have you accepted financial pressure, lack, debt and even poverty as a normal part of life?**

Maybe you have a history of poverty or lack in your family, a long streak of lost opportunities, or debt that seems insurmountable. These are all areas of attack the enemy uses to dethrone God's people from their position of dominion. If you've been in the world of lack and poverty long enough, it may have become a way of life for you—something you can't seem to push past in your expectations.

I have good news! No matter what your situation—you can have all God desires for you in the area of finances, and you can take financial dominion. You can be debt free, live in the overflow, give extravagantly and rise to new levels. God gives you the power to get wealth because He made a covenant with you to do so (Deuteronomy 8:18).

The principles detailed throughout this book are the same principles that have worked for me and countless others I have mentored through the years. They have resulted in very successful wealth creation journeys and I desire the same for you!

My Beginning

I started as a clerk in Local Authority, I eventually rose to a management position, but I still **BELIEVED that there was more to me** than making ends meet. So, I started **digging with questions**. Everything in life starts with a question and conversation that first begins in the mind!

In my book, *The 5 W's of Wealth Creation* I discuss the process to wealth creation called the APPA principle. This is where you start with asking questions, planning and preparing before taking any action in creating wealth. The more I did, the more I discovered who I truly am, why God created me and what I already owned in the spirit realm that I needed to force down to the physical realm by asking, seeking and knocking for it. I was not idle and refused to accept the status quo. This changed my **ATTITUDE** and the way I thought began to evolve.

I knew I was meant to own land – real estate; this is all part of what the Creator has given us. I always saw the pain of masses of people going to the council for assistance as they found themselves homeless. I felt moved and wanted to do something. So, I started asking the right people, 'How can I do it?' In order to answer that question, I needed to first answer the question of, 'What do I have in me, and what are the opportunities around me now – that I can start with?'

I quickly discovered that managing my income was crucial, so I built the **HABIT I term ESSA: E**arning more, **s**pending less, **s**aving more to **a**cquire assets **(ESSA)**. Yes, I had a job, but I also wanted to create multiple streams of income by building a successful property portfolio. I educated myself and went for training in the area of mortgage brokerage. I became a qualified CEMAP all the *while still having my 9 to 5* job and a young family to raise. As soon as I'd get a little bit of savings together, making use of the leverage around me – I took **ACTION**, used the savings as a deposit and purchased my first home to let. (My full story, available from Amazon, can be found in my book *Successful Property Investment: How I turned a £5k loan into £15m in assets.*)

If you can change your mind, you can transform your life. You see for me, it all started with believing and changing my attitude. I had to learn more, focus and refuse to accept what seemed like impossibilities. My attitude was like that of an eagle and I soon learned how to ride the storm. All of this led to positioning myself to create the necessary habits. I developed the habit of learning, not despising small beginnings and not giving up. I worked on my *mind* first and began meditating on thoughts of who I truly was. I encouraged and *inspired* myself by having a picture of where I wanted to be and reading books about those who had already got there. I networked with other like-minded individuals and I had a relentless desire to reach my goals.

I hope that my story inspires you, please know that the *starting point to unlocking wealth is acquiring the right knowledge and applying the necessary principles*. As you continue to read and apply what you learn, you too can discover the hidden wealth available to you.

Chapter One
BELIEVE

"If you believe you can, you probably can. If you believe you won't, you most assuredly won't. Belief is the ignition switch that gets you off the launching pad."
- Denis Waitley

Principles

I spend a considerable amount of time mentoring people, from various walks of life, <u>who</u> desire to create wealth. The common denominator with every single person I have mentored is their <u>*MIND.*</u> I have been able to pinpoint a person's ability to succeed or fail based on what they think and how they think.

Mentorship is like extended education and it has many benefits for both the mentor and those mentored. The secrets to wealth creation are simply principles and philosophies that few have chosen to practice and adopt. These principles are the foundational subjects I start all of my mentorships with.

The outline of principles listed below, will help you create multiplication and abundance when utilised correctly. Each principle is reviewed within the book in further detail, but I wanted to begin by giving you a snapshot of what's to come and what will be required of you.

I must first say that I am not a financial adviser, but below are *my principles* outlining the steps I took to transform my life; if they have worked for me then they can work for you too:

1. The **BAHA** Principle envelopes and undergirds everything.
2. The **ESSA** Principle applies to how you manage what comes to your hands!
3. **TIIE** -The Four Devils of Investment (Tax, Inflation, Interest rate and Exchange rate.) Watch out for the Four Devils when you invest.
4. **FRESH** Principle. This is a principle that helps you invest wisely so your investments are hands-off.

5. **RIB** – you must build an investment pillar I call RIB. (Real Estate, Investment and Business)
6. **ALIE** – These are the four keys required to focus, monitor and measure your finances, you must be certain to review your finances with these keys. Ensure you understand what it means to do the following:
   a. **Assets: You must strive to acquire assets**, that diversify into different asset classes.
   b. Liability: Identify the **liabilities and ensure they are** reduced or negated altogether.
   c. **Income** must be multi-stream. Always strive to have your income derived from assets rather than physically working for money! This way you can earn while you are sleeping.
   d. **Expenses**: This should be an essential of life! Your expenses must be managed, measured and monitored so they do not become liabilities!
7. STAR Investor: Ensure you are a STAR INVESTOR. Strategise, build the right TEAM, take timely ACTION and expect realistic RETURNS.

Hidden Wealth can be viewed as a self-help guide developed through the accumulated notes, observations and advice I have used to mentor others over the years. It is my desire to bring some of the benefits of mentorship to you through this book. So, let's start at the very beginning!

Whenever I undertake a mentorship session, I always start with the **BAHA** Principle which stands for:
1. Believe
2. Attitude

3. Habit
4. Action

In the coming chapters, we will review each step of the BAHA Principle in detail. For now, I will outline the four steps to provide a general overview.

Every principle starts with what we **believe** (who we are and what we have). We are able to develop our beliefs to form the **attitude** of a champion who may go through debt, illness etc. but will always make a success of things and triumph in the mind. Then, we develop **habits** through our routine to get us to the destination of abundance and we begin to take **action** and act accordingly.

The first two points, belief and attitude, are key and relate heavily to your ability to RECOGNISE WHO YOU ARE. This is done by understanding YOUR IDENTITY in your mind first. You must be able to have a clear picture of who you are, what you have AND what you must do with what you have. The clarity of this picture in your mind will determine how far you can go.

Believe

A belief is a mental attitude that terms a proposition is true. The Oxford Dictionary states that to believe is, 'to accept as true or real: to have faith in someone OR something.'

Belief is all about your mindset and deals with knowing who you are in Christ; understanding who you truly are, i.e. your identity, will bring clarity and focus and shift your mindset to that of a wealth creator.

In this context, I believe all human BEINGS created and alive believe in something or someone – that is the way you were created! The word BEING in this context means, in my view, to BE IN G(OD). You are not an **accident;** you were **created by God** and so you are **in** Him. The success of your being depends on believing in your creator God, therefore the first step to unlocking your hidden wealth is to believe in **who** God created you to be. You must also understand what your mandate is which is to be fruitful with the potential He has loaded within you – multiply it to replenish the earth, subdue it and have dominion.

You will be able to unlock your wealth if your **being** is **alive** in who you are, Whose you are, what your mandate is and what you need to do with that mandate. This in turn helps you form the positive attitude of a winner just like eagles and lions. Irrespective of who you are and what your condition or situation is at present – whether you are unemployed, employed, in debt or just making ends meet.

What you believe will translate to what you think, see and say about yourself.

An **eagle** *believes* he is a survivor and can ride storms even though eagles are not the biggest birds. Likewise, a *lion believes* he is the king of the jungle and *sees* himself as a champion. He sees **food**, not fear, when he sees other animals and he **talks** by roaring. He does not compete – he is fearless! An eagle is fearless to the storm and glides through it. You too must approach the business world and wealth creation with this fearless attitude of courage. Do not give up until you discover, develop and dispense the ability, potential, and talent that God gave you to bless the world with when He first created you.

You see, all human-BEINGS were created by God to **BE-IN-**God (BEING). You may think you came from your mother, but in the book of Jeremiah God says, 'Before I formed you in the womb, I knew you, and before you were born I consecrated you; I have appointed you...' You are not an accident. There is purpose to your life and God has blessed you with abundance; all that is left is for you to unlock the blessing of creating wealth without sorrow for you and your generation. Some have money but they also have plenty of sorrow, sickness and stress with it. This is not the kind of abundance I am talking about. When I refer to abundance, it is an abundance that comes with no stress or sorrow. Don't add sorrow when creating wealth by trying to do it all alone and in your own strength. Instead, be guided by the Holy Spirit in you, the voice of God, so your being is alive in Him for direction.

If you are reading this today, *know for sure that you believe in something or someone – this is the way we were all created. There is no free thinker!* You have to be in Him who created you and knows you more than anyone else – including your parents, friends or spouse – to unlock the supernatural wealth I am talking about. God has put the seed of greatness in you.

Man is the only one that was formed by the hands of God! The rest of creation - God spoke into existence! That shows how much He loves and believes in the seed He gave you to create supernatural wealth. You are surrounded by **opportunities which can sometimes come in the form of problems that you or your generation face.** The more problems you can solve with ideas the Creator gave you, the more wealth you will be able to create. If you solve the problems of a million people you will become a millionaire; a billion problems solved will make you a billionaire. The story of Colonel Saunders the founder of KFC has always been a motivator for me when it comes to turning problems to opportunities which create lasting wealth.

Success stories usually start as a problem. Colonel Harland Sanders was unhappy with the 35 minutes it took to prepare his chicken in an iron frying pan, but he refused to deep fry the chicken, which he believed lowered the quality of the product.[ii] If he pre-cooked the chicken in advance of orders, there was sometimes wastage at the day's end.[iii] In 1939, the first commercial pressure cookers were released onto the market, mostly designed for steaming vegetables.[iv] Sanders bought one, and modified it into a pressure fryer, which he then used to fry chicken.[v] The new method reduced production time to be comparable with deep frying, while, in the opinion of Sanders, retaining the quality of pan-fried chicken.

In July 1940, Sanders finalised what came to be known as his 'Original Recipe' of 11 herbs and spices and as discussed later in this book KFC is now a $15billion industry with almost 20,000 locations globally in 123 countries and territories as of December 2015.

Who, What And Why?

As a mentor, I always include the foundational principle of asking questions to see if people know who they are. The internal perception you have of yourself will lead you to the position you occupy externally. Believe you are a created being designed to create abundance with the potential you have inside. Ensure you have the attitude of a person who does not despise small beginnings.

You must focus and have a vision. Plan where you ought to be AND APPLY PATIENCE UNTIL YOU REACH YOUR

DESTINATION. If you are on an airplane flying to a specific destination, you don't tell the pilot to hurry up just because you want to get there fast! You sit and wait patiently, even when faced with storms and turbulence – you are asked to put on your seatbelt and you obey, why? It's a matter of time, your destination is fixed. Life works in the same way, you just have to cooperate with the Creator, obey His commands, use what He has given you and you will arrive at your destination!

Believe you are **who** He created you to be. You are a creator like your Father! All of the provisions you need are already available to you in this world, and in you, in the form of ideas, with the potential to create abundance! God is not going to create anything new – that is what He created you to do. He has equipped you with abilities, ideas, imagination and a powerful mind. Never forget that you are a CREATED BEING. God has given you unlimited, unique potential hidden within you – that is your 'what' and it comes in the form of ideas, capabilities and talent. *Why did He give you these precious things*? He gave them to you so that when you discover and developed them, you will be able to *dispense them and bless* others. This blessing is not just for you, your family and community – but the whole world!

Now we will look at the most important area when it comes to potential: where you plant your seed (i.e. the ground on which you plant) – potential, ideas, your mind – will determine whether your <u>seed of potential</u> will grow. The seed is perfect, it's the soil of your mind that must be conditioned to enable the seed to be fruitful. So, what types of soil are there and how can we make sure we plant on good soil the perfect seeds of potential we have been given? Let's look at the different kinds of soil. You see, your mind is likened to *four different typical kinds of soil that exist.*

The Soil Of The Mind

Soil is important, Matthew 13 tells of the parable of the sower where seed is sown in different types of ground. We learn that it is seed planted in good soil that yields fruit.

A tree planted in good soil will yield good fruit in all seasons. It must be good soil to ensure you have multiplication and abundance that lasts. The parable talks of four different types of ground. You may be sowing your potential and abilities but are your seeds being planted in the right soil? (Matthew 13:3-8):

1. Planted by the wayside: seed on the wayside is always eaten up by birds or stepped on. It is exposed too early; it has too much exposure to the sun without the roots first being able to fully form – you do not profit from sowing in this type of ground. The wayside is where most people are; it represents the status quo kind of employment and vocational roles where you are comfortable but going nowhere. *The wayside is a place where there is too much traffic* which tends to slow you down, you will not find your significance in this type of soil! This can also translate to the state of your mind; until you get out of the box you can't grow and multiply.

2. Planted on stony ground: seed sown on stony ground will produce a bit initially but because it is not rooted, it will not last or multiply and increase. Stony ground reminds us of places where there is *too*

much opposition – this may be in the form of systems, location, employment, vocation, profession and people. Stony ground is where your potential won't be recognised!

3. Plated on thorny ground: thorns choke the root and prevent it from growing. This represents acquaintances, comfort zones, family background, culture or mindsets where you compete with others in your career for places and positions, for example, instead of focusing on your unique abilities to complement and be a blessing to people. *Thorny ground is an environment where there is too much competition and stereotyping but nothing is produced* – thorny ground places or mindsets won't help you produce any fruit. **This type of soil chokes your ideas as they spring up**, the **ground represents opposition to your ideas**, you will have opposition from systems, people, laws and legislation, delays etc.

4. Planted on good ground: this is where your potential can grow, *where there is a prepared place for you, where your seed of ideas, potential and gifts will manifest into fruitfulness*. Good ground is where you need to sow because it is good ground that will yield harvest and multiply your seed sown.

It does not matter where you are now – in a vocation, i.e. job, making ends meet or in your profession where you are skilled on your career – just make sure you are not by the wayside where there is too much traffic or on stony ground where there are obstructions. You do not want to be on thorny ground with systems opposing your potential. Good ground is where you should sow your potential because it will grow.

In the next chapter we will discuss the best place to plant your ideas, gifts and potential in order to unlock your abundance so that you can be a blessing to yourself, your family and the world

Hidden Wealth

Chapter Two
MIND MATTERS

"Your mind is a powerful thing. When you fill it with positive thoughts, your life will start to change."
- Anonymous

"Our life is what our thoughts make it."
– Marcus Aurelius, Meditations

Planting The Seed – The Mind Leads The Way!

The mind is a furnace of your thoughts.

As a man thinks, so he is - as you think so you are: poor or wealthy! It's a choice of what you believe. For you to transform from poverty and lack to wealth and abundance you need to pay attention to your thoughts.

Transformation is first a thought before it becomes an action and the process starts from the mind.

Your mind leads the way to the life you live. I believe this is the reason why, under normal delivery, a baby's head comes out first when the baby is born! This emphasises the reason why the mind is important.

Did you know that 75% to 95%[vi] of the illnesses today are a direct result of our thought life? As well as our bank balance, what we think about also affects us physically and emotionally.

The average person has over 30,000 thoughts a day. Research shows consciously controlling your thought life is one of the best ways to change the way you think and transform your life. It allows you to get rid of damaging thoughts which consume your mind and control your life.

Negative thoughts are thoughts that do not produce positive emotions, choices or outcomes. Our minds consume so much that is unnecessary. If we could learn to only say and think what's needed, then we would be so much more productive.

Change in your thinking is essential to transforming your life. In order to consciously control your thought life, you must refuse to let unhealthy and negative thoughts destructively run riot through your mind.

You must learn to actively engage with each and every single thought that you have, analyse each thought and then accept it or reject it: keep the 'good' and reject the 'bad'. Actually, most of us don't mentally engage with our thoughts, especially whilst performing routine tasks, and engaging is so important!

Renewing

Do not be conformed to this world, <u>(their way of thinking and doing)</u> but be transformed by the renewal of your mind, that by testing you may discern what is the will of God, <u>(which is to be a wealthy and healthy)</u> what is good and acceptable and perfect.' - Romans 12:2 ESV *(underlined amplifications added)*

When you renew something, you give fresh life to it, you revive and strengthen it. No one else is responsible for renewing your mind. You and you alone must take responsibility to change your mind.

If you have spent 50 years of your life thinking a particular way – you do not have to spend the next 30 years doing the same thing. A poverty mindset can be transformed into a mind that produces wealth and abundance.

Let's look a little closer at the renewed mind. The word 'new' in Greek means 'new in time' like a brand-new car or something that is 'new in quality.' Everyone, irrespective of their age, can have a mind that is new in quality.

Don't copy the behaviour and customs of this world but be transformed into a new person by changing the way you think. Then you will learn God's will for you, which is good, pleasing and perfect.[vii]

To renew your mind, you must review the following areas: Motives | Identity | Network | Decisions

M: Motives

Thoroughly examine your motives as it will bring to light any wrong thinking that needs to be changed. Why you do what you do will be directly linked to why you think what you think.

I: Identity

Changing the way you think requires a change of identity. Seeing yourself differently goes hand-in-hand with thinking differently about yourself. It is also about the lens with which you view the world around you.

N: Network

The brain has a 'network' which forms each of your thoughts. Changing your thinking, is changing your network. When you renew your mind successfully, you are literally changing your mental blueprint.

D: Decisions

Renewing your mind and changing the way you think is a choice that will affect all of your other choices; from your financial choices to your relationships and everything in-between. Right thinking means better decision making.

Feeding Your Mind

William Durant, an American writer, once said, 'The trouble with most people is that they think with their hopes or fears or wishes rather than with their minds.'

The mind must be used intentionally and actively. If not, you will find that your emotions are the driving force when making decisions.

What have you fed your mind today through the gateways i.e. your eye gate - what you see, your ear gate - what you hear or listen to? It is important to think about the books you read, the TV shows you watch, the podcasts and messages you listen to, the people you engage with and the food you eat. If you can take the time to notice what you are putting in, it will be easier to identify what negative things need to be replaced.

Are there people around you that you share your dreams with or bounce ideas off? Identify your 'core group' and how their input and responses impact you.

Evaluating your thoughts is key. It has been stated that we are bombarded with 4000-10,000 ad messages on a given day[viii]. That means we are exposed to thousands and thousands of words, concepts and thoughts. Self-defeating thoughts do not just come from nowhere. You must take note of what you are taking in.

Ideas Rule The World

Never forget that _everything created begins with a thought_ or an idea and ideas are the birthing ground for greatness. Below, are a couple of examples showing how some have managed to create wealth with their ideas:

Two young men came together in their spare time to build personal computers. They had an idea of transforming technology as people knew it and, as a result, created the worldwide tech juggernaut we now know as Apple. Steve Jobs and Steve Wozniak had ideas which, coupled with motivation and action, developed into a company that has reached a net worth of over $1 trillion!

Kevin Systrom and Mike Krieger, the founders of Instagram, created a check-in app but had the idea to incorporate photography because of the increasingly popular smartphone cameras. They saw a need, an opportunity – and created a solution to problems, that impacted millions, with a change in technology. Systrom and Krieger started from a rented desk in a shared office – working on evenings and weekends when they weren't at their day jobs. At first, their idea didn't really go anywhere as the sharing of mobile photos was not as popular as it is today. When they changed the focus of the company to almost entirely mobile photography, the app took off. Two years later, Facebook bought the company for $1 billion.

All of the top companies started with ideas, they recognised problems and opportunities, and used their potential to unlock wealth – you can too!

Mind exercises are so important because they provide you with ideas and ideas really do rule the world!

Every day, new scientific and technological advancements are being made that have the potential to change the world we live in. It's all part of the new 'Innovation Economy'.

In recent years there has been loads of new technology that will impact our world in the future. From driverless cars to driverless airplanes! The way we shop has definitely changed, causing many top companies and well-known retailers to close down. Think of Debenhams, ToysRus, Homebase etc. But, on the flip side, the new technology has meant that other businesses have emerged and taken advantage of the changes in technology; Amazon is a great example of this. Over the next century, the innovation economy will affect the way we shop and the way we pay for our shopping. It's been suggested recently that Cryptocurrencies are the future, but this is just a small part of the possible changes. In truth, there is a <u>*more powerful 'currency' being spent... IDEAS!*</u>

In order to create wealth you need to have wealth-creating ideas. And you don't have to look far because the ideas you need are all within you. In my book, *The Five W's of Wealth Creation*, **I discuss important questions everyone must ask in order to create wealth. I discuss how to turn £5k into £15m in another of my books titled,** *Successful Property Investment*. **If you desire to create wealth, I encourage you to get these books on Amazon.**

What problems can you see around you? If it's a problem to you then it's definitely a problem to millions of others; you may just have a solution if you think hard enough!

That is your moment of opportunity!

Once upon a time, **Mark Zuckerberg** had a good idea. Now that idea is called Facebook and he's worth about $60 billion. Jack Dorsey also had a good idea to help his struggling company. That good idea became Twitter and Dorsey is now a multi-billionaire.

In this new innovation economy, good ideas are directly linked to wealth. What does that mean for you? Well, it doesn't mean you need to invent the next Facebook or Amazon - not everyone will be able to do that. I never will, however, I believe that everyone can create abundance in their lives and enjoy wealth as a side effect of the ideas that they create, and that includes you! Your Creator said He would give you nations for your inheritance and open the windows of heaven to you. Windows are for illumination – light and ventilation! God is saying He will give you ideas because ideas are birthed where there is light and illumination.

Please stop being a slave to other people's bad ideas. Instead, turn the ideas of your mind into great ideas that create wealth by unlocking the wealth inside you and believing in who you were created to be.

God is not in control of your abundance, He has given you the provision, raw materials, to create your wealth. Your provision is your POTENTIAL, creative ability and authority! You have the power to create abundance; it's a matter of choice – are you willing to find out what your potential is, discover it, develop it and dispense it? You choose, you make the decision.

All you really need to do is receive what He has for you and follow His instruction.

Wealth

We now understand that everything begins with the mind. The most important thing about the mind is that it can be changed! Several years ago, I decided I was going to learn how to get wealthy and I quickly realised it was my mindset that mattered the most.

Benjamin Franklin once said, *'Without continual growth and progress, such words as improvement, achievement, and success have no meaning.'*

Do you know you can believe anything you want about wealth? Don't allow yourself to be limited by your beliefs. You can create any amount of wealth you want for yourself. You'll need the principles and knowledge of how to do it, but before you can get to the tactics and strategies of how you do it, you must first have the mindset for it.

Being fully aware of what your current wealth beliefs are is part of the first step. If you can identify your beliefs, you can question them and then make the necessary changes to create a better future.

Time and opportunity are valuable resources that should not be wasted. Although time can be exchanged for money, if you believe that your time is only there to create money, you will always be trying to trade your time in exchange for money. This means you will work physically from 9 to 12 midnight trying to earn money! But, if you believe that the value you create and exchange produces money and provides services and products from your creativity to solve the problems around you – then your focus will be on how to provide value, which in turn creates your wealth.

You can only make money in two ways; either through an exchange of your time or from assets that produce returns without you. This small difference is everything for creating wealth. *<u>You should always strive for your income to ultimately come from your assets rather than physically exchanging your time for money, otherwise you will be trapped as an earner instead of having a return on investments which work while you are asleep</u>*. There is only so much you can physically do and there are only 24hrs in a day. Time cannot be preserved or extended!

You will need to identify where your beliefs about wealth and wealth creation stem from; this is how you become aware of what your mind has been thinking.

Most people don't have an intentionally set wealth ethos or philosophy. You need to think intentionally about how you desire to view wealth and wealth creation for your life. This way, you can proactively create the financial life you desire.

Remember, what you think and believe about wealth will determine the actions you take towards creating it, and as a result, will determine whether you are able to take financial dominion. If you desire to change the financial results you have, you must first change how you believe and what you believe when it comes to wealth and wealth creation.

The Word Or The World

There are two ways of creating wealth: The world's way,

where you toil day after day and night after night, relying on living from pay cheque to pay cheque; in the end, you have little to show for your labour. Then, there is the way of your Creator. I am talking about the word's way – The word created the planet we live in. Wealth created the word's way is wealth that adds no sorrow to it. God's way is without stress as long as you believe in Him, believe in who He says you are and follow His instructions.

If you choose to follow the way of God's word, then you will not only transform the way you think but you will also transform your attitude. Let's take a closer look at the importance of attitude in the next chapter.

Hidden Wealth

Chapter Three
ATTITUDE

"Attitude is a little thing that makes a big difference."
— Winston S. Churchill

"Attitude is a choice. Happiness is a choice. Optimism is a choice. Kindness is a choice. Giving is a choice. Respect is a choice. Whatever choice you make makes you. Choose wisely."
— Roy T. Bennett, The Light in the Heart

Hopefully, it has now been ingrained that the picture of who you are begins in your mind. From your mindset, you cultivate your attitude and behaviour. I discuss this fully in my book *The 5 W's of Wealth Creation.*

Attitude

So, the first step is to **believe** who you are, form a **mindset** of who you are and what you have, then build the **attitude** of a champion; a winner who is fearless, focused and vision oriented.

Your attitude will always reflect your mindset. A focused person who is able to create wealth should:

1. Have a *long-term view attitude.*
2. Possess the *attitude of a learner,* and be inquisitive (desire to learn more – seeking mentorship from those who have already been where you want to be).
3. Plan and prepare (this is always done before taking action). Have the attitude that nothing happens unless you make it happen – <u>*if it's going to be it's up to me!*</u>

<u>Your attitude is a choice which stems from your beliefs and until you change this, you cannot begin to create wealth!</u>

"Nothing happens until the pain of remaining the same outweighs the pain of change." - Arthur Burt

Your attitude is all about your standpoint. It is your perspective that concludes how you see things and how you respond to them. Where you choose to position yourself is linked to your beliefs and the way you think and feel about any given situation. Your attitude matters! It is what triggers your habits and ultimately, your actions.

*I once read a **story of a Prince** who was given an assignment to go undercover and learn about the suffering of a poorer area within his nation. The Prince had to live with the poorest tribe for a month so he could understand how best to help. So, off the Prince went - he travelled to the area, mixed in with the tribe and lived in horrible conditions that were unimaginable for a prince. After two weeks, one of the tribe members asked the Prince, 'Why is it that you don't look miserable like the rest of us?' The Prince answered, 'Because I know who I am, and this is a temporary place and condition for me!' The tribe member laughed and mocked his answer, but the Prince did not reveal who he was. One day, an enemy attacked the tribe and began asking those captured who they were. It was the enemy's prideful plan to contact family members of those captured and inform them that their loved ones had been killed. The Prince was the first one to be called and he said, '**I am** the Prince of this country and I am **here on assignment**. I have an undercover army who are guarding this place...' Before the Prince could complete his sentence, his royal army swamped the place and killed the enemy. They delivered those that had been captured and the Prince was able to complete his assignment and send the needed aid.*

The above story clearly shows that the **Prince believed in and knew who he was, what he had and what his position and assignment was; he knew his current condition was only temporary!** What a great attitude in the face of great danger around him! The Prince believed in who he was, he believed he was royalty, even when he was living in a slump. Do you **know** who you are? Do you **see** who you can become and are you declaring it by **saying** it?

As mentioned before, to discover your hidden wealth as described above, your attitude must be likened to the attitude of an eagle or a lion. Eagles are not the biggest birds, **but** they believe they are and have the attitude of being the greatest in their environment, this translates in their actions within their environment. A lion is not intimidated by the biggest animal like elephants or the fastest like cheetahs. Nor are lions the tallest like giraffes. Likewise, eagles, who are not the biggest birds can see far, fly high and are always prepared. They have the capability to ride a storm. They are focused and have a symbol of tranquillity.

These two animals have great attitudes. Even though a lion is not the biggest, fastest or tallest animal in the jungle, when he sees an elephant, he does not think of his size the lion is thinking of food! When the lion sees a cheetah, he does not desire to run like one; the lion is majestically steady and confident – with no fear.

What you believe you are, and the picture of who you are on the inside matters if you are to unlock your hidden ability. How you see yourself truly matters as it will determine your attitude, habits, actions and how others see you.

If you are to unlock the hidden wealth inside you, believing who you are must translate in to how you carry yourself – it must impact your attitude. Don't be fearful of any challenges you encounter; don't take flight, rather hold on and fight. Hold on to your beliefs of who you are and be sure to focus on the destination even if your environment changes! You must view every challenge as an opportunity, embrace change, persevere, have a vision and set goals strategically flexible enough to accommodate change while still focusing on the destination of creating wealth to bless your generation.

In the UK, many are worried about the financial climate of the nation, but they need to stop thinking about the negatives and use their minds to create wealth through ideas.

For example, I always say, 'Whether there's Brexit, no Brexit or a hard Brexit; people still need a roof over their head.' My response has always been:

'In the whole scheme of things, Brexit will be another footnote to history in a decade. We have survived the oil crisis, 20%+ hyperinflation in the 1970's, mass unemployment in the 1980s, interest rates of 15% in the 1990s, the global financial crash in 2009; whatever happens, happens. People will still need houses and a roof over their heads. If property values drop, it is only a paper drop in value because you lose when you sell. Long term, we aren't building enough homes, and so, property is a long game no matter what happens – the property market will always come good.'

That is the attitude and stance I choose to take!

"A challenge you face is an opportunity invitation for change!" - Elizabeth Benjamin

The attitudes I encourage you *__to get rid of,__* among others, to unlock wealth are:

- The attitude of **complaining**
- The attitude of **blaming**! Until you do this you will not leave your current situation. Some blame their parents, school teachers, their race, their education and even their politicians!

Build the **attitude** of **fearlessness, courage** and **boldness. Have a long-term view of reaching your destination** in the midst of a changing environment and external changes.

The world we live in will always change; these changes can create opportunities to create wealth if you just look hard enough. Wealth creation begins when you are able to think and find an answer and solution to the problems around you. The more people you solve problems for, the wealthier you become.

Just like the Prince, our lives are driven from what we believe in; the picture of who we are inside is paramount because it will determine the **attitudes** we have which in turn produce our **habits** and ultimately our **actions**. So, if you believe you have been created to be a creator with unlimited potential, ideas and the capability to produce and create abundance then no matter what happens – you will still be able use opportunities to create wealth and be a blessing to this generation.

Mindsets Form Attitudes

A mindset can be defined as the established set of attitudes a person has; mindsets reveal how people think and bring to light a person's belief system – why they think the way they do. If you don't like your attitude, then you must check your mindset.

Your mindset is the foundation because your mind works like fertile ground awaiting seeds to be deposited. If you desire to produce something of value, then the soil must be clear of debris and anything else that may tarnish and hamper growth.

If you desire to unlock hidden wealth, then you will *need to transform your mind*; this can only happen when a mind shift has taken place. The process of a mind shift is no different to the four stages a seed goes through in the ground: I call this the four D's in my book *Creating Wealth from Within*, where I discuss the concept fully.

There are *four D stages a seed goes through*: The starting point for a farmer or the planter is to clear the **debris** before planting.

1. **Dig:** Just like a farmer digs before planting, you must prepare your mind for the shift and transformation or in the case of a builder who requires a solid foundation before building – they often need to dig out the dirt first. This is where most of the work takes place; digging out all the junk of mistaken identity and thoughts of who you think you are – which were formed by the environment you live in or come from. You must also dig out some cultural mentalities, upbringing, and education which are

contrary to who you are created to be.
2. **Depth:** For a seed to survive and be transformed to fruit, the soil has to be deep enough to protect the seed from the sun and surface flooding etc. this will allow the root to form in strength and produce fruit. Real depth is required for transformation. It cannot be surface-level change. A farmer knows that if he desires to plant, he must first clear the soil of debris and dig deeper. When seed is planted in shallow soil, there is not enough soil for the seed to anchor its roots. In the case of a builder, the stronger and bigger the building that is erected – the deeper the foundation must be. Otherwise, if a storm comes it won't be able to stand. So unless you dig deeper into your heart for a solution to the problems you can see around you, you will just settle for mediocre worldly opinions of others who think it's impossible.
3. **Darkness:** At first, seeds are planted in the darkness of the soil to allow them to form strong roots before they are exposed to light. In the same way, your solution starts in the dark area of your mind. It's the darkness of your pain from the past and bad experiences you are going through or have gone through that help you give birth to your breakthrough, as you dig your thoughts away from your current situation. It's in the darkness of our lives when no one knows our pain that our value is formed and character and competence are built!

The thoughts and great ideas you have inside you are at first not visible to the naked eye. The thoughts of possibility and solutions to problems around you will soon start to emerge into the limelight. As your mind begins to process it, you can start to put your ideas into practice – then you are on track to becoming limitless. If you can learn to shift your mindset to focus on the possibilities of the potential in you, it will come to fruitfulness that translates into producing a service to bless your generation.

4. **Death**: Seeds go through death to their form and SIZE! This is so they are able to grow into fruit. The ideas to solve the problems you see around you had to first die to their thought-form before translating to great products and services. As you start to die to your past complaining and blaming attitude, and take hold of the truth; you possess what it takes to create wealth irrespective of opposition. If you make the decision to emerge with a new attitude, then new habits and actions will follow. So focus on positive ideas born out of your pain, and set your mind on its possibility; process it, believe it, think it and see it.

Make use of the opportunities around you so that you can be trained and skilled up in the necessary areas of your potential and giftings. Get educated, network with other like-minded people and take timely action. The ideas you have will start to transform and develop into products and services that solve bigger problems which can touch millions of people and generations to come. Every product you use started with an idea in someone's mind! Never forget that ideas rule the world.

Hidden Wealth

Chapter Four

HABIT

"Moral excellence comes about as a result of habit. We become just by doing just acts, temperate by doing temperate acts, brave by doing brave acts.

We are what we repeatedly do. Excellence, then, is not an act, but a habit."
-Aristotle

Your daily habits are what will either help you to achieve your goals or confine you to a mediocre life.

What are your daily habits? Are they success orientated or mediocre?

'Good habits formed at youth make all the difference.' - Aristotle

'Chains of habit are too light to be felt until they are too heavy to be broken.' - Warren Buffet

First we form habits, then they form us. Conquer your bad habits, or they will eventually conquer you. If you can break your bad habits and focus on developing good ones you will simplify your life. *'The ability to simplify means to eliminate the unnecessary so that the necessary may speak.'- Hans Hofmann*

If you change your beliefs and adjust your attitude but fail to address your daily routines and habits, you will see little to no growth or change.

Ultimately, it is your habits that will help you achieve – the vision and actions of <u>wealth</u> creation will then follow. Every successful person can trace their life success to a routine they establish for themselves. Routine is the invisible path to a future you desire. Once you set up a destination you must create routines – **habits** that get you to your destination of success.

Mohammed Ali was once asked if he liked waking up at 4.30am to run in the morning. He replied, 'I hate it, but I love being a champion!'

Habits

The <u>*secret to wealth creation*</u> will be hidden in your <u>*most consistent habits*</u>. Take a look at the wealthiest people in the world and you will find a common trait; they are all people of habit.

If you are in poverty and living from pay cheque to pay cheque, then feeling sorry for yourself won't change your situation; it is the **habits** you form that will.

Dale Carnegie summed it up when he said, 'Feeling sorry for yourself and your present condition is not only a waste of energy but the worst habit you could possibly have.'

Consistency is key, a change in your daily habits may be all that you need to kick start your wealth creation journey. Consciously create habits because habits unconsciously dictate your life.

Amongst other things, wealthy people think big, they are tenacious and never stop learning. They are masters at what they do and know how to set and achieve goals. You will find tremendous benefit by adopting the right habits.

The Oxford dictionary defines a habit as, 'a settled or regular tendency or practice, especially one that is hard to give up.' Every successful person can trace what they have built to their routine.

Habits are routines formed over time. They are practiced, regular and repeated tendencies that eventually become a part of your make-up. Once you know your destination and have a goal to create wealth you then need to develop the right habits to get you there.

People form habits all of the time – even without realising it. It is easier to do than most think in the sense that all you need do is continually practice something. Consistency is key – because of this, habits are often formed in the negative sense rather than the positive. Some have habits of spending all they earn; they cannot go out without buying what is not needed!

You must be intentional about the habits you form – this is done by reviewing and assessing your beliefs and attitudes.

Routine is a powerful path that will help you propel your vision INTO THE FUTURE and make it become your reality.

David had a routine to worship; Daniel had a routine of praying three times a day. What is your routine? Routines should always be created with a focus on vision, goals and mission.

Forming Habits

If you desire to form the right habits to unlock your hidden potential, then there are certain routines you must follow. You will need to develop some of the habits listed below, among other positive habits, to unlock the hidden wealth in you:

- **Develop the habit of learning**: always seek knowledge and understanding in the area of wealth creation. Ask the right questions that will help build your understanding.

- **Develop the habit of managing time wisely:** time is valuable. You cannot buy it back so it is vital you learn how to effectively use and maximise the time available to you.
- **Develop the attitude of not despising small beginnings** – count every penny and the £'s will take care of themselves. I called this habit the ESSA Principle.
- **Develop the habit of a saver.** This means saving from all income that comes to your hands, no matter how small it is. It's the consistency that matters so avoid wastage at all costs. If you can't save from £1 you won't save when you earn a million as your habit will be to spend all you earn!

The ESSA Principle

I refer to the ESSA Principle as one of the key principles, it simply means: **E**arn more, **S**pend less, **S**ave more and **A**cquire assets.

The ESSA Principle is required in managing what comes into your hands to build the future you want. In short:

1. Earn more i.e. create multiple stream of income, look for ways to increase your income.
2. Save more to invest.
3. Spend less.
4. Acquire real assets not just perishable items and stuff that devalues.

These four habits will help you manage what comes to your hands. Your income is a seed and it's how you manage it that determines the wealth you can create. Let's look at them in further detail:

EARN MORE: Never limit your income to a pay cheque. Even if you are currently in a 9-5 role, with no sign of promotion or advancement, there is always opportunity to increase your income.

You are more valuable than you realise! Look at your skill set, what are you good at and what gifts do you possess? Is there something you do well, or find easy to do that others don't? If so, you can charge for it. You may be in a position where a second job is of benefit for a short period of time. The additional income could provide you with the necessary funds to get started.

Are you good with hair? Then become a hairdresser in your spare time for extra cash. You could tutor or sell things, bake cakes etc. The options and possibilities are endless. Your goal should be to build multiple streams of income.

SPEND LESS:

Prioritise and only spend money on the essentials such as your tithe, bills and transportation. Before spending money on luxuries, first reduce your liabilities. This is not just about getting rid of debt; ***it is about managing your overall spending habits.***

Learning to spend less money by prioritising on the essentials is paramount to creating wealth and is something you must do. Cut out the unnecessary and avoid wastage. The daily coffee's and takeaways are not necessities. Look at your expenditure, identify all of the non-essentials and delete them from your spending. The majority of what most people spend their money on are often cosmetic, unnecessary and unimportant things to their survival; if you can live and function without it then it's probably a non-essential!

SAVE MORE: It goes without saying, but if you can learn to spend less then you will be able to save more. The less you spend, the more you have available to save.

Proverbs 13:16 says, 'A wise man thinks ahead; a fool doesn't, and even brags about it!' Learning to save is learning to think ahead. We are told in Proverbs 21:20 that the wise store up choice food and olive oil, but fools gulp theirs down. Saving is a wise thing to do!

Learning to save is a habit you should adopt immediately. Don't despise small beginnings, if you can only save £50 a month then begin there. It's not the amount that is of most significance, it's is the principle. With any income you receive there should always be seed (enough funds) to plant again for your next harvest.

As you save, you will be able to acquire assets. Open a 'wealth' account by arranging a fixed amount to save each month that you will use for investments. By doing this, you can train yourself to save from your income and not your leftovers! If you do not plan to save and put the money away instantly in preparation for investing, you may find spending tends to increase because you don't have a goal for your money.

Please note, when I refer to saving, I am talking about

saving with a purpose – hence why I call it a 'wealth' account and not a savings account. Generally, saving is only putting money aside for short-term use, like a rainy day, but investment is setting money aside to grow – for long-term use.

<u>ACQUIRE ASSETS</u>: You should not just save to store up funds in your bank account earning next to nothing, that would be pointless and yield very little return. *You should save so that you can acquire assets and build a wealth creation portfolio.*

Good assets should; be of value, produce value and increase in value. They should appreciate and work to your advantage.

- **Develop the habit of exercising your mind with positive thoughts:** Don't just exercise your body but learn to exercise your mind. Learn to actively think, be deliberately creative and learn to strategise – developing and looking for solutions.

Mental exercise must be exercise that includes meditation on who you are and what you have. It is your responsibility to inspire yourself!

I discuss taking medicine for the mind if you want to create wealth in *Creating Wealth from Within*.

Mindset Medicine

We have already discussed the mind and mindset in previous chapters but what I would like you to focus on here is what I call your 'mindset medicine.' By this I mean the habits and routines you must form to ensure your mindset is one of a wealth creator:

<u>Meditating</u>: Meditation has been given a bad reputation in many circles but there is nothing mystical about it. The Bible tells us in Genesis 15:5 that God told Abraham to look at the stars to see how numerous his descendants would be. To meditate is to simply think on something over and over until you have a clear picture of it.

<u>Inspiration</u>: Create an environment where you can inspire yourself, this will help you avoid worry and the stresses of life.

<u>Networking</u>: Network with like-minded people who are going where you are planning to go. Pay attention to successful businesses that have achieved what you desire or take some time to view the type of house or car you want to own for inspiration. Link up with a team of professionals so you are able to delegate what you are not gifted to do.

<u>Desire</u> and dedication: You must have the desire and dedication to succeed. Sow into the life of others and develop the habit of giving because giving is living. Life is worth nothing unless you give of your talents, gifts, money and service to others. Expectation is key, have a positive outlook towards life and expect that when you invest you will have a reward. Be thankful and have an attitude of gratefulness no matter the situation you find yourself in. Know that even the challenges you may face are a steppingstone to your breakthrough to higher ground in the journey of life. Sometimes your struggle is a recipe for your success.

The right beliefs, mindset, attitudes and habits will be of little value if you do not take action. Success is in the 'doing' and the next chapter will show you exactly how to act on what you have learnt to ensure it works for you.

Chapter Five
ACTION

"God provides the wind, but man must raise the sails."
—ST. AUGUSTINE

"The path to success is to take massive, determined actions."
—TONY ROBBINS

The final step in the BAHA Principle is all about putting everything into action. Once you believe in who you are, what you have and what you need to do then you can change your mindset, adjust your attitude and create a routine and transform your habits; you must take **action**.

'Do not wait to strike till the iron is hot; but make it hot by striking.' – William B Sprague

Take Action

If you do everything there is to do but fail to take action then you will ultimately fail. Action is the process of doing something – meaning taking action is something you must do. Activity and movement – 'doing' – are required for achievement. If you desire to accomplish any endeavour then you must become a person of action.

God will only bless the work of your hands so you have to do something because He will not bless nothing.

It is what you do with what God gives you that will determine whether it will multiply and grow into abundance. When it comes to your finances, you always have an income which is seed; how you manage that income (seed) determines your increase.

In a previous chapter, we have seen that to be alive you must believe (be-live) in something or someone. Every human being has their being in what they 'be-live.' Your beliefs foster your attitude; it is from your attitude your habits are formed and from your habits you **act**.

Mankind lives, moves and has their being in the direction of

<u>what and or who they believe. All those living must be-alive meaning all be-live. If you are alive then you must 'believe' in something and whatever you believe in is what you become. This is why mindset renewal is the foundation of wealth creation.</u>

You must believe in:

1. <u>Who</u> you are - A created being.
2. <u>What</u> you have - Unlimited potential.
3. <u>Why</u> you have it - <u>To be a blessing to your generation.</u>
4. <u>Where</u> it is - Deposited in your heart. The soil of your heart i.e. the mind needs to be renewed and fed with the imagination of who you are daily, so that you can have the desire to discover develop and dispense!

Understanding the above is like someone being told they have a possession worth millions, but it has been hidden in the ground somewhere and they must locate it. The first thing that person will need to do is have a revelation of what is hidden and its true worth. They will need to know how and what they need to do to get to it. This means understanding the required resources and tools needed.

Then they will need to clear all of the debris from the soil to get to their precious hidden possession. Because they know the true value of the possession, they won't allow anything – external elements, forces or otherwise stop them from accessing it.

Where Wealth Is Hidden

So where is this hidden wealth and how do you take action to unlock it? The answer is…it's hidden in your heart. *To unlock it, you must:*

START FROM THE INSIDE OUT

- *Start with **asking questions**. Interrogate your mind for the solution to the problems you can see around you!*

When you ask the necessary questions, you force yourself to think productively, *this is clearing the debris from your mind.* Your mind is like soil that has been fed with all kinds of philosophies and education that does not line up with who you really are! You need a mind shift so that you can have the mindset of the wealth creator you have been created to be.

- **Exercise** you mind by thinking positive thoughts and developing good ideas that provide solutions to the problems around you! Think about the future, what problems can you see and have you got a solution? By this I mean, do you have ideas? Because your ideas will produce the solution.

As we now know, wealth must first be created on the inside because your actions will always follow your thought life.

Effective thinking is an exercise of the mind and heart and requires intentionality. It's like *digging* for diamonds; once you locate the correct thought you refine it, clean it and dust it off. Like diamonds and precious jewels – your thoughts must be kept securely, and your mind looked after.

It's easy to say get rid of the junk but how do you rid yourself of toxic thought patterns? It may seem like a very simple question to answer, but it's worth noting when it comes to the mind – what you put in will determine what you get out.

If you feed your mind junk, then junk is what it will produce. If you feed your mind negativity, then it will produce negativity. Negative thoughts and junk-filled minds are easy to pinpoint because of what they produce.

- You **must replace negative** and toxic thoughts with positive thoughts of who you are and what you can do. This will come when you intentionally:
  1. Take time to think about what you are actually thinking about.
  2. Respond to negative thoughts with words of affirmation. You must realign your thinking and provide a new direction for your thoughts to travel in.
  3. Fix your eyes and ears before what you desire to become or have in your life and not on what's contrary to it.

By doing these things, you will start to believe the pictures you have created of who you are and who you desire to be. Once you believe who you are and what you have then you can move towards reinforcing thoughts that you can be wealthy. Your whole being will have no choice but to move in the direction you point it towards.

- **Meditation** for mindset renewal works in the same way. Meditation helps you see things as they should be and

enlarges your viewpoint and perspective. To get to a hidden diamond in the ground, you need to first **know** you have something precious. With imagination and meditation – you must focus on:
1. What you are worth
2. What you can become
3. Your desires
4. Networking with those who will assist on your journey

Remember to be expectant! If you don't expect change then you won't recognise it when the opportunity for change comes and things will remain as they are.

- **Knowledge; <u>what you know</u>:** Neil deGrasse Tyson, an American astrophysicist, author and science communicator once said, <u>'Knowing how to think empowers you far beyond those who know only what to think.'</u>

I am sure you have heard it said that we are in the information age where, *'we are learning more than we understand and understanding more than we know.'*

Knowledge is not power because power is nothing without control; ***<u>applied knowledge is power</u>***. Too much information, without an outlet or something that facilitates the opportunity for growth, development and understanding is, in essence, useless. Learning and education are key too, you can always learn from others. Before planting, a farmer will need to learn about the seed he desires to plant. He must understand what type of soil and conditions will help the seed grow. Learning and education work in the same way.

When you position yourself to learn and be educated, you position yourself to grow and increase. Your knowledge expands, and your understanding is elevated.

Daniel is a brilliant example. The book of Daniel 5:14 tells us that Daniel was found to have insight and intelligence and wisdom like that of the gods. He was renowned for his wisdom, knowledge and understanding. Daniel was even wiser than the experienced magicians and enchanters of the kingdom![ix]

Like Daniel, if you desire to unlock hidden wealth then you need to *increase in knowledge, wisdom and understanding and learn about wealth creation and investment products.*

Whilst what you know is very important, who you know can also be of great significance. Having the right relationships in place is key.

- **Building healthy relationships; who you know**
  Connect and network with healthy relationships that aid you on your journey, helping you to grow your ideas. Improving your understanding in the area of your passion and mission is paramount. ***God did not create us to be independent or dependent on anyone except Himself. However, He does expect us to be interdependent because we need each other!***

We are all busy but busy does not necessarily mean productive! More importantly, very few of us, no matter how busy we find ourselves, are living beyond mediocrity and achieving the kind of wealth we desire or achieving the goals we set for ourselves. Figures such as the ones below begin to make sense when we view them in light of this:

1. 80% of businesses will fail within the first year and a half of starting.[x]
2. 26% of us have no emergency savings, whatsoever.[xi]
3. Around 4-7% of people are able to quit smoking on any given attempt without medicine or help.[xii]

Remember – true success is never an accident, and lasting wealth creation is a deliberate journey. You must prepare for it; this means choosing the right thoughts and bringing them to life.

- **<u>Understanding risk and return</u>**

The state of your mind will determine how you invest and create wealth. You need to be a lion or eagle type of investor. Forward plan and ***<u>don't be afraid to invest</u>***. There is no need to fear or get emotional when making decisions, just ensure you acquire the necessary knowledge and understanding before making any kind of investment.

There is nothing like no risk, but you can measure risk and go for something that is low, medium or high risk. The parameters of each risk level will always depend on the individual and what they have at their disposal.

I would like to stress that if you invest, it is a good idea to think with the mindset of the MAXIMUM you are willing to lose and the minimum you are able to gain.

The Principle Of Action In The Business World

Learning the right principles in the business world is the first step to action before investing or creating wealth.

The *following principles* show the next step after you clear the debris from your mind and educate yourself in the business world of investment. The principles below need to be learned and adhered to in order for you to become a smart investor and create wealth.

The BISE World Principle: Learn, understand and make a shift.

Understanding where you are in the business world will help you know where you need to be. Where are you right now? To help you answer this, below are the four main classifications of where most people are in their working life. Once you have identified where you are you can begin to make the necessary shift for creating wealth. Your current working life will fall into one the following categories:

1. Vocation
2. Profession
3. Passion
4. Mission

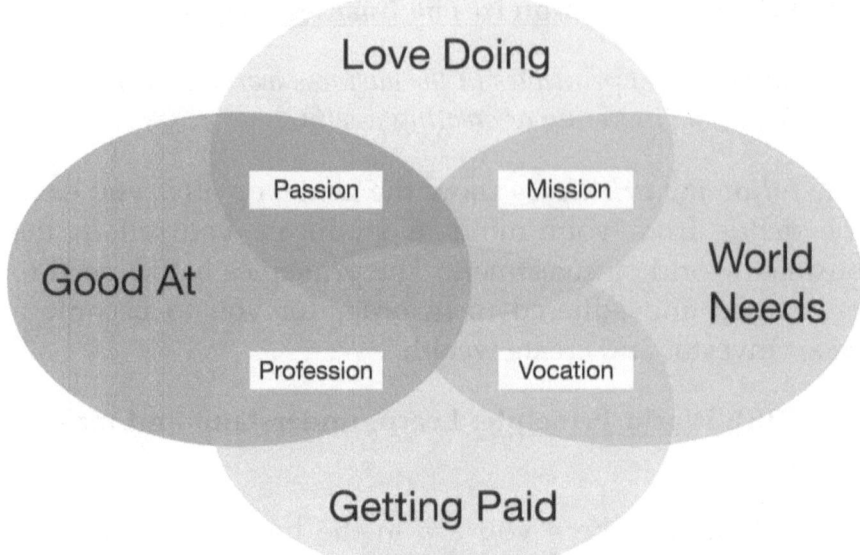

Your **vocation** is your job, it is generally what you **'have to do'** to make ends meet for income. This is where most of us start from. Your vocation is just a J.O.B: just over broke! A vocation is not necessarily where your potential is or what you love to do. It's a means to an end.

Your **profession** is your career – what you **are trained to do or good at.** Again, this is not necessarily what you love to do and it does not always highlight where your potential is. You could be trained to be a mechanic or a doctor, but your potential may be in singing or acting!

Your **passion** is what you **love doing**, whether you are paid for it or not! It comes from your heart even if you don't receive monetary benefits.

Your **mission** is something you **give back to the world**. It is an important assignment or commission – something that the world, community and those around you need *from your potential*.

To unlock your hidden potential, you will need to shift to your passion and mission if you are to create true wealth. There is nothing wrong with starting a vocation or profession, but ***your passion is a pointer to you what your potential is and unless you recognise it,* you** will not be fulfilled or make use of that potential in creating wealth.

There are four main areas of focus in the business world:

1. Business
2. Investors
3. Self-employed
4. Employee

Most people are either employed or self-employed, some run a business, but the majority have failed to step into the world of investment and business.

The majority within **vocations and professions** are usually in the classification of employment, where they work for somebody else or have employed themselves through self-employment; their 'time' is still employed. *There are limitations within these two sectors* because you cannot live forever, and you cannot be in several places at one time. This means you cannot make wealth while you are sleeping or no longer in existence and as a result you cannot create lasting generational wealth!

Most prestigious professions, for example footballers and other sport professionals tend to also have the limitations of age against them. Once a sports professional reaches a certain age nobody wants them! Unless they shift their focus to business and investment with the money they earn while they are in sport, they are likely to become poor.

The business and investor world are where you can create lasting wealth. There is no limit to what you can create and there are no age barriers! Earlier, I mentioned the Kentucky Fried Chicken founder, Colonel Harland Sanders, who made a discovery of 11 herbs at the age of 50 - that eventually made KFC a global enterprise.

Born in 1890, Sanders discovered the 11 herbs in 1940. It made KFC the second largest restaurant chain in the world[xiii] – after McDonalds – operating in more than 21,000 locations across 118 countries. KFC has a franchise revenue of over $23 billion and the net worth of the market capitalisation of its parent company is estimated to be around $28.3 billion (this figure also includes Pizza Hut and Taco Bell). At present, the fast-food restaurant chains net worth is estimated to be more than $15 billion[xiv].

The restaurant has won many awards, yet Sanders – the man behind this fried chicken empire – was once considered a failure by others as he only achieved mediocre success in what he did previously. It took Sanders 40 years to prove himself and in doing so, he showcased to the world that success can knock at your door anytime.

His journey is one of the greatest stories of determination and shows there is no barrier of age when it comes to creating wealth through business or as an investor.

Owning a business, or businesses, is where you need to make the shift to as it can ignite your income, perpetuate wealth and holds many benefits for you, your family and, when done correctly, will enable you to bless the whole world. Businesses can go international – your services and products can be a blessing all over the world in places you may never physically go to. A successful business can also enable you to help people you may otherwise never meet personally. This is why it is essential you learn and understand how to become an investor; it will take your income to another level of abundance.

Take a look at the book of Psalms:

Blessed is the nation whose God is the LORD, The people whom He has chosen for His own inheritance. - Psalm 33:12

Please understand I am not encouraging you to chase money. God should take first place and be Lord in your life. To be blessed means you are empowered to prosper, Psalm 33:12 tells us that God has chosen for His inheritance those who will have Him as their Lord. The wonderful rich and vast earth is the Lords and the fullness thereof – now that is true abundance!

You were created to touch and transform nations – this is not possible by simply working a 9-5 and having just enough. Abundance is not a greedy or selfish concept. It enables you to bless and empower others around you, transforming nations and generations.

ALIE Principle: What you should focus on to build wealth.

The ALIE Principle is akin to building the trunk and branches of your wealth tree to enable lasting continuous fruit that will multiply and last generations. Just like the life of fruit on a tree is dependent on the life and strength of the trunk and branches, these principles are vital components if you are to create lasting wealth that will stand the test of time!

You must understand the ALIE Principle, which refers to:

1. Asset acquisition
2. Liabilities
3. Income
4. Expenses

One of the most important principles when it comes to achieving financial freedom is to learn the four main areas of action you must be aware of so you can monitor, manage and measure at all times. These areas are like four entrance points. You need to constantly watch out for, as they determine whether you will create lasting wealth or create generational debt and poverty.

It does not matter how much income you earn in your vocation or profession or what kind of profits you make in your business or earn from investments, if you don't master these doors which are the points of entrance, i.e. the necessary action required for each door, then anything that comes to your hands as income and profit will soon disappear and you will not be able to create lasting wealth.

It has been said, 'it's _not what you make that matters it's what you keep to grow that creates wealth._'

To take action, you need to focus on the following areas:

1. ASSETS: You must plan, prepare and save to _acquire assets_ no matter what your income is at present. In Genesis 12: 1-3 God told Abraham to step into supernatural wealth and abundance. God said this would happen after Abraham got out from his country, kindred and family; _then go_ to the LAND (this signifies your assets) that God would SHOW him. Likewise, you must get out of your old mindset – your wayside, stony and thorny soil environment. The result will be that God will make you a great nation and bless you so you become a blessing! Once you have the mindset of a wealth creator, you need to know what you should focus on. God said to Abraham I will give you land! Land is something that will grow – having assets helps you perpetuate wealth.

We will focus more on assets further on and look at what assets are and how to diversify, **proportionally, into asset classes that work without you!** You will discover how to ensure you build a strong pyramid and how to include foundational bedrock investments. I will also explain passive assets that produce income whether you are alive, sleeping or have passed on, and active asset high velocity assets that bring higher returns without you physically working for it, that can be passed on to the next generation's assets.

2. Liabilities: A **liability**, in financial accounting, is defined as the future sacrifices of economic benefits that the entity is *obliged* to make to other entities as a result of past transactions or other *past* events,[xv] the settlement of which may result in the transfer or use of assets, provision of services or other yielding of economic benefits in the future.

A liability is defined by the following characteristics:

- Any type of borrowing for improving business or personal income that is repayable during short-term or long-term periods;

- A duty or responsibility to others that entails settlement by future transfer or use of assets, provision of services, or other transactions yielding an economic benefit, at a specified or determinable date, on occurrence of a specified event, or on demand;

- A duty or responsibility that obligates the entity to another, leaving it little or no discretion to avoid settlement; and,

- A transaction or event obligating the entity that has already occurred.

In summary, liabilities are _**what you OWE and not what you OWN.**_ They usually attract charges which are added to what is owed, this means that the lenders are in control. Debts that you don't reduce or negate quickly may keep increasing and when what you OWE is more than what you

OWN, you will be in debt and poverty. The Bible says in Proverbs 22:7 that the borrower is servant to the lender!

You must watch your liability doors. To do this you must use the **3M's: Measure Manage and Monitor**. I expatiate on this in my book *Wealth Within*. You are to manage, monitor and reduce by focusing on <u>reducing or negating your liabilities</u> all together so you are able to create lasting wealth.

3. Income: This may be in the form of **earned income** i.e. wages, salaries or **returns** from assets you own.

The two main focuses of action to concentrate on are the sources of your income and the fact that your income must be multi-stream in nature. You must strive to ensure the sources of your income are from assets you own, and they must be multi-stream. This means returns must be from other gifts (abilities) you have, other assets in the form of diversification to asset classes i.e. bedrock foundational base, passive and high velocity assets. Have diverse pillars that uphold your pyramid. We will discuss the principle of **RIB and wealth pillars** later in the next chapter.

4. Expenses are the essentials of life not the luxuries of life. Essentials usually include what you cannot live without. The main areas I refer to include food, shelter and clothing. This can comprise of things like paying for your rent, mortgage, utility bills, tithe (as a Christian 10% of your income/returns), tax (most are deducted from the source if employed!), holidays (I do not necessarily mean the holiday of a life time where you borrow money for it, as this will then mean you are increasing your liabilities). Your focus

on this door must be *to ensure you budget for your essentials. Manage your spending wisely, use your income to pay your expenses from your income and not from borrowed money. This will increase your liabilities* especially when you borrow money on credit cards to buy groceries! You must manage your expenses wisely; don't buy things unless you need them.

PILE Principle: Financial freedom – first steps to create lasting wealth.

PILE means (Passive Income Liability Expenses). This is my formula for calculating what financial freedom means. Financial freedom means different things to different people. You need to understand what financial freedom means to you. To aid with this, there are three questions I ask my clients once they have the mindset of wealth creation.

You cannot create wealth unless you can cater for your needs and are finically free to cater for your needs and family and ensure you have a retirement plan for when you are not able to work. Once you pass this stage then you can look into creating generational wealth to pass on. So, let me ask you:

1. What does financial freedom mean to you and how can you create it?
2. Retirement: When do you want to retire (from the 9 to 5, self-employment or employment) and how much do you want to retire on?
3. What is your current/existing net worth and what do

you want it to be in the future? Your net worth is what you will pass on to your generation when you are not around. Net worth is all assets minus your all your liabilities.

Understanding these three areas will help you focus on the principles and apply them in creating wealth.

My definition of **financial freedom is** *when your* passive income = living expenses.

When the income from your assets is equal to your living expenses (mortgage, rent, bills, holidays, family essential expenses etc.) then you are financially free!

As you can see this does not mean you first need to have millions in the bank to cater for your retirement plans or have a robust net worth. *The PILE Principle is the first step to wealth creation* and means you can cater for yourself and your family without physically working or exchanging your time for money. However, you still have to create lasting wealth and abundance that reaches generations to come.

If you can programme your mind to the idea that you don't physically have to work long hours to make money, then you will begin to think about investments and your eyes will be opened to the investment opportunities around you. There are only 24 hours in a given day and there are only a maximum number of hours you can work each day.

Once you are financially free, you must ask yourself exactly what you are free to do? In a nutshell, the answer is you are free to create abundance that positions you to then take care of so much more than you and your lifestyle. You can create the kind of wealth that lasts generation after generation and impacts multitudes!

So exactly what is the **difference between financial freedom and wealth creation**? I liken the difference to someone who needs water and has to go out in the rain to collect it with their hands; each time they go out, they get wet and it becomes a tedious task as they must collect for themselves and their loved ones. Eventually the person is promoted from using their hands to using a bucket and having a tank in the home for storage. However, whilst this is a vast improvement from collecting rain with their hands, it is not the ultimate destination. Eventually the rain will stop, and the tank will be empty; this is where all those in employment and self-employment are.

The easiest way to define financial freedom is through your passive income and living expenses. I call this the *PILE* figure (Passive Income Living Expenses). Passive income is income or return that comes from your assets and investments. It is not generated from you physically exchanging your time to earn, i.e. working a job. Jobs are limited – when you don't have a job, you are unable to earn money. Successful passive income allows you to make money whilst you sleep. Although we call this income, the correct term is actually a return from your investments and assets that work without you! Your financial freedom figure equals your PILE figure. Real financial freedom is when all your living expenses are met by passive income.

In some ways, to some people financial freedom is a destination. It is reaching a certain level of wealth where you no longer need to concern yourself with how you will pay your bills or ensure you have enough cash at the end of the month. Financial independence is exactly that; it is being free of the burdens of finance; it is having options.

Going back to the analogy of collecting rain, wealth is <u>having a WELL in your home that is linked to the ocean!</u> It is a place where you have sustained the continuous uninterrupted flow of water; you are not impacted by the weather, lack of rain or other external influences. After all – an ocean doesn't run dry like a stream does!

Your wealth creation steps should look like this:

Financial Insecurity: Your journey begins from financial insecurity where the majority of people are i.e. where you can't pay your bills in full because your expenses are more than your income! You are always in shortfall every month.

Financial Security: The security stage is where you break even. Your income equals your expenses so there is nothing to save or invest!

Financial Independence: Independence is where you are free i.e. PILE; Passive income = Living Expenses. In other words, the assets you acquire are producing income that is more than your needs.

But this is still not the wealth creation that I am referring to as you have a mission to leave a legacy, so you need to move to the next stage.

Financial Abundance: At this stage, your passive income is now in abundance, enabling you to help others. We then arrive at the final stage.

Financial Legacy: This is where your income not only touches others but has a generational impact, view the five levels of wealth creation diagram – it all starts from acquiring assets!

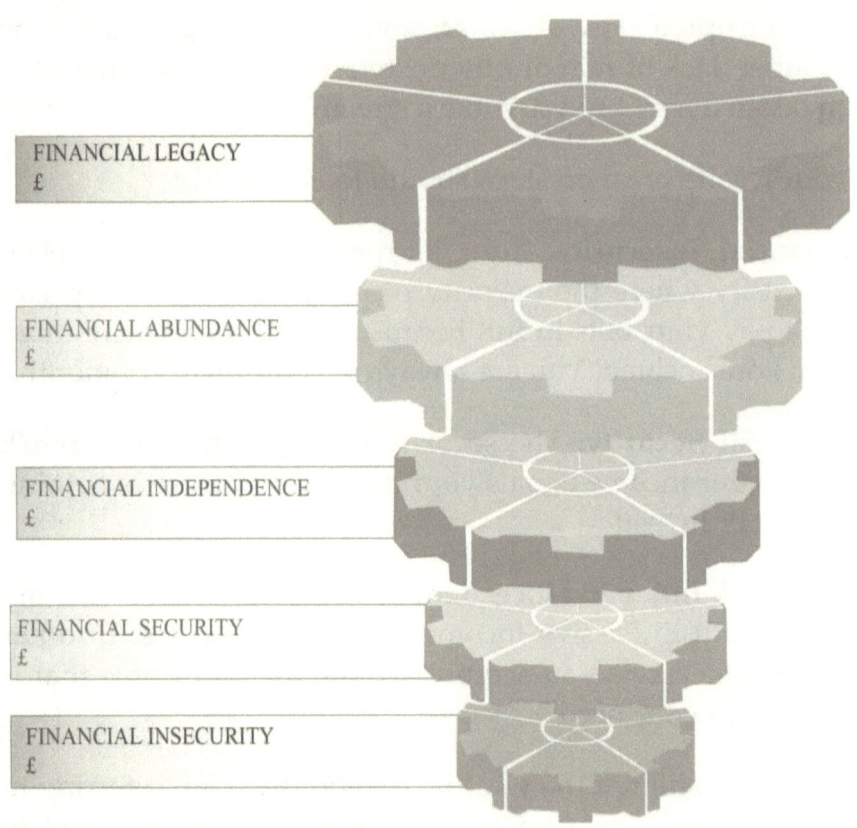

FINANCIAL LEGACY
£

FINANCIAL ABUNDANCE
£

FINANCIAL INDEPENDENCE
£

FINANCIAL SECURITY
£

FINANCIAL INSECURITY
£

Assets

What is an asset?

An asset is anything of value that can be converted into cash. It can be something tangible or intangible. There is a simple way to easily understand the difference between a tangible asset and an intangible asset.

Tangible assets are akin to physical assets that are not consumed during the course of the business. Buildings, land or cash are all examples of this.

Intangible assets are non-physical and include things like the brand name or the website.

Asset Classes And Diversification

Asset classes are different categories of investments such as stocks, bonds, and cash – including cash equivalents, real estate and derivative investments.

An asset class can also be known as a broad group of securities or investments that have similar financial characteristics. *This can be direct and indirect investment.*

Traditionally, the four main categories of **asset classes** are:

1. Cash
2. Shares
3. Property
4. Fixed-interest securities (also called bonds)

Mixing different asset classes is called **diversification**.

Diversification helps you manage the amount of risk you take with your portfolio. It is vital that you learn how to diversify your investments when it comes to wealth creation; especially when trying to create wealth in unstable environments.

Make sure you **diversify** with a different mix of **asset classes** as below. As your wealth grows you must be able to have the correct pyramid structure of the asset classes:

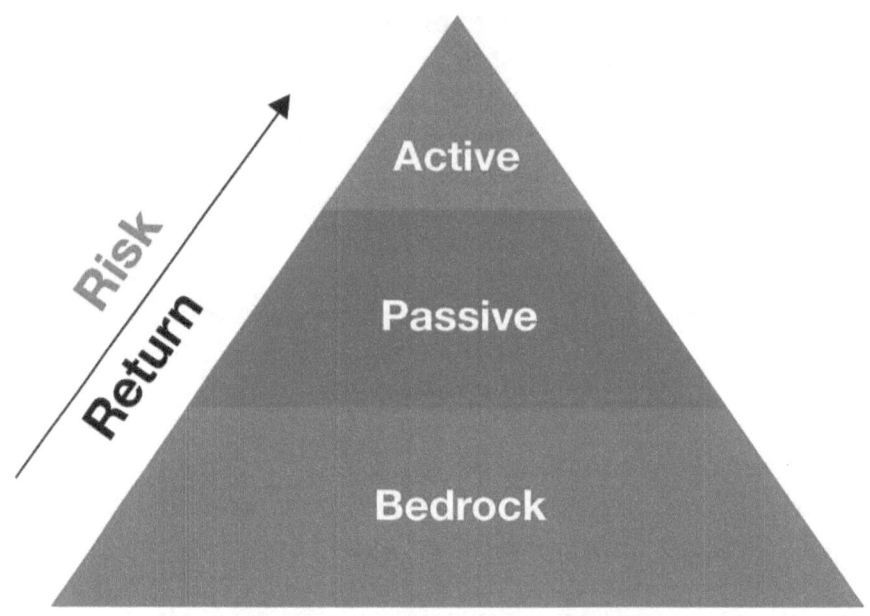

Look at the features of each asset class and review the positives and negatives before you actively invest.

Bedrock assets are low risk investments. They include things like cash, collectible metals like gold, fine arts, wines and low risk government bonds, ISA's and pensions. Bedrock assets usually help you hedge against inflation. It's advisable to keep at least 30% of your net worth in asset classes, especially as we enter a new phase of uncertainly in the market when inflation is rising and cash value is falling!

Gold – As of late, records show that gold prices have been on the incline in comparison to the pound sterling. The expectation is that while Brexit negotiations are going on, and in the future, sterling will be subdued for the coming months as the parliamentary stalemate plays out. This suggests it's likely that investors will continue to back gold bullion as a less risky investment option.

Passive assets – Passive assets are assets that produce passive income meaning once you own and possess them and you can receive returns from them without having to physically work on them. These types of assets are usually for medium to long-term and are **medium risk**. They include residential (this includes buy to let, HMO's (Houses in multiple occupations) and commercial real estate investments, including car parks, garages shops, student accommodations, petrol stations, dementia care homes, holiday homes, hotels, and other buildings).

Active assets are high velocity and **high-risk**. These types of assets are usually short-term investments that produce high returns and carry a higher risk. They include **bonds, shares, loan notes, forex cryptocurrencies etc**.

You must allocate your assets appropriately and in proportion of your portfolio – grouping each asset into the relevant classes.

Although there are a wide range of assets, as described

below, you must be able to allocate them in a balanced way. Understanding each asset class and its features will help you appropriate effectively so you have a robust pyramid which can withstand any market.

Chapter Six

PILLARS OF WEALTH CREATION

"Many folks think they aren't good at earning money, when what they don't know is how to use it."
- Frank A. Clark

"Money is multiplied in practical value depending on the number of W's you control in your life: what you do, when you do it, where you do it, and with whom you do it."
- Tim Ferriss

Pillars Of Wealth Creation: The RIB Principle

To create wealth, you must rid yourself of all the preconceived notions you have about wealth, your finances and opportunities for investment. Wealth creation really is a simple process that merely requires the understanding and implementation of a few key foundational principles.

Creating wealth is like constructing a building, once the foundation is built, you start constructing pillars that will hold the structure of the building to ensure it is strong and able to withstand the weight of the building.

In wealth creation, there are three main pillars, which I call RIB, you should aim to include in creating wealth:

There are numerous written types of wealth creation pillars ranging from 7 pillars, to 5 and 3 which include things like: Debt, i.e. leverage income from a career, intellectual assets which are products of your ideas – for example books, songs, paintings etc. Other pillar versions include things like marketing investment and online trading as pillars. However, I believe all of the above fall under one of three main categories, because unless you invest income or make use of your equity/leverage to invest in at least one of the three areas listed below, you will not be able to create lasting wealth. I have coined the pillars RIB because like human ribs protect vital organs; the three pillars are also vital in a financial sense. They provide the resources needed to build.

R Real Estate	**I** Investments	**B** Business
Commercial / Residential Land and Buildings	Loan notes Bonds Shares Savings ISA's Pensions	Set up business Sell business

The **pillars of wealth** creation ensure you diversify across a wide range of asset classes. As mentioned, they include investment, real estate (which includes land) and business. Let's take a closer look at each one:

Real Estate

There are four main types of real estate:

1. Land (green land and brown sites)

2. Buildings i.e. (residential, for example houses and apartments)

3. Commercial properties which consist of industrial **real estate investments**. This is everything from industrial warehouses leased to firms as distribution centres over long-term agreements to storage units, car washes and other special purpose real estate that generates sales from customers who temporarily use the facility. **Retail real estate investments** consist of shopping malls, strip malls,

and other retail storefronts. In some cases, the landlord also receives a percentage of sales generated by the tenant's store, in addition to base rent, to incentivise them to keep the property in top-notch condition.

4. Industrial real estate investments often have significant fee and service revenue streams, such as adding coin-operated vacuum cleaners at a car wash, to increase the return on investment for the owner. **Mixed-use real estate investments** are those that combine any of the above categories into a single project.

Investment

Investment: Anyone can be an investor; all that's required is having the mindset of an investor and an understanding of what it means to invest.

It's worth repeating that while saving means putting money aside (either under your bed or in a bank etc.) for the short-term expenditure on perishable goods or a fancy holiday; investing means putting money aside to grow <u>for long-term purposes.</u>

<u>Investing has to be for medium to long-term periods, this helps you benefit from compound interest.</u>

One of the main benefits of investing i.e. putting money aside to grow long-term, as opposed to setting money aside to spend for day to day expenses and rainy days which is what most saving accounts are to many people, is because of compound interest.

Generally, **compound interest is** what most of us deal with in our savings, investments and loans. It is interest calculated on the initial principal and also includes all of the accumulated interest of previous periods of a deposit or loan. This basically means that you are earning money from the interest you've already earned.

The diagram below shows the benefits of compounding investments over longer term periods.

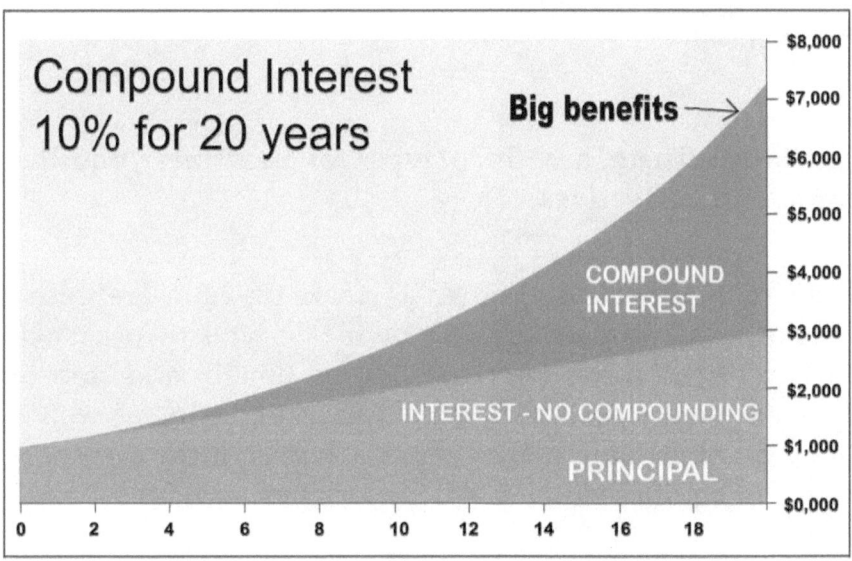

There are an array of investment opportunities to choose from. As the diagram above shows, *compounding* returns are powerful and the earlier you start the greater the advantage. Money can have increasing value over time if you know what to do with it.

Although the word investment covers broad areas including assets, an investment portfolio or pension fund may include a range of different asset classes. Here's a quick guide to what they all mean.

Cash: Cash is simply cash, held in a savings account. It will deliver low growth (only at the best rate of interest that can be found) but is very low risk. For this reason, it is often included in portfolios and funds as a 'safe space' in which to store gains that have already been made. The only significant risk of cash is that it can gradually lose its value due to inflation.

Securities: There are three types of securities; **equities, bonds** and **derivatives.**

Equities: Equities, also known as stocks or shares, represent a stake in a company. If you own one, you own a small portion of the company. They can be bought and sold on stock exchanges and their value fluctuates, losing as well as gaining value. This makes them a high risk in the short-term, but equities are best suited to longer-term investment.

Bonds: Bonds are essentially loans, either to governments or corporations, which are paid back over time with interest. They range from low-risk (e.g. UK government bonds, or gilts) to high-risk (bonds issued by a company raising money will depend on that company's health), but on average they are lower risk than equities. They tend to provide steadier returns and fluctuate less in value.

Derivatives: Derivatives are complex investment products, to be approached only with caution (and following professional specialist advice). The value of derivatives is based on ('derived' from) the performance of another type of asset.

Commodities: You can invest in a wide variety of physical assets, ranging from farm produce such as grains to gold bullion. All are known collectively as 'commodities. Investing in commodities is relatively high risk, and they tend not to deliver as much growth as securities either. So why invest in them? The advantage of commodities is that their performance is completely independent from that of securities – meaning that they can help to balance a portfolio by offsetting the risks and cushion the potential losses from securities.

Collective investments: If you're keen to invest in a range of different types of investments, but you don't have the time or the knowledge to pick your own portfolio, a collective investment could be a good option. With this type of investment, your money is pooled with other investors' and then invested across different asset classes.

OEICs: An OEIC, or Open-Ended Investment Company, sells shares in the company itself. It then invests money to buy assets on your behalf, and the performance of the investments affects its share price. Different OEICs offer different levels of risk and potential return depending on what they invest in, so it's worth consulting a financial adviser before deciding where to put your money.

Unit trusts: If you invest in a unit trust, you buy units of a fund which is run by an experienced fund manager. The manager picks the assets to invest, based on their view of which investments are likely to perform best. Depending on your investment goals and timeline, an independent financial adviser can help you choose the right unit trust for your money.

An asset class can be defined as a broad type of investment, as mentioned above, which in summary includes:

1. Cash
2. Bonds
3. Shares
4. Bonds and property, or
5. Investing in several funds
6. Commodities which classify mainly in three areas:
    a. Metal – Gold, silver etc.
    b. Energy – Gas, oil etc.
    c. Agricultural - Livestock farming

Stocks and Shares ISAs: A tax-free way of investing in shares or investment funds, up to an annual limit.

Many unit trusts and OEICs come pre-packaged as ISAs. Alternatively, you can choose for yourself which investments and funds to put in your ISA.

Workplace pensions: A way of investing for the future, with a contribution from your employer and tax relief from the government. Your money is invested in pooled funds.

Personal pensions: A way of investing for the future, with tax relief from the government. You can use it instead of or as well as a workplace pension. Your money is invested in pooled funds.

Investment bonds: A life insurance contract that is also an investment vehicle. You invest for a set term or until you die.

Endowment policies: A life insurance policy that is also an investment vehicle. It aims to give you a lump sum at the end of a fixed term. Often you choose which investment funds to have in your policy.

Whole-of-life policies: A way of investing a regular amount or a lump sum as life insurance. It pays out on death and is often used for estate planning. Often you choose which investment funds to have in your policy.

Businesses

Whilst the benefits of business tax advantages are positive, you can also touch more lives globally by setting up a business with your products and services. There is a level of impact you are able to achieve through owning a business. When you are self-employed, you still need to work for yourself rather than operating a business which has a set up system that can work itself without you physically needing to work in it.

In my experience, to set up a business you have to go through seven planning and preparation stages which include the following:

    1. Decide what type of business i.e. Complete a

SWOT analysis - What are you good at?
2. What problems are you providing solutions to?
3. Research who your clients or customer will be.
4. Identify your competitors.
5. What is the type of business in legal terms? I call this 'name it' i.e. ST, LTD etc.
6. Finance – This can be achieved through savings, family and friends, partners, ventures, alliances, bank finance etc.
7. Location (shops, online etc.)

Now all that's left to do is start!

There are eight types of business set up, the one you choose to start will depend on your individual circumstances as each business type has its own benefits depending on your personal circumstance:

1. Sole trader – this is the oldest form of trading there is, it's also the simplest and most common type of **business** you'll find. The clue is in the name – meaning that you are solely responsible for everything the **business** does and you're often known as the proprietor. This is the usual form for small shops and **businesses** that provide services such as beauticians, hairdressers, photographers, gardeners and so on.

When you start out in **business**, most often you use your own money to fund the venture. However, as you start to grow, you may need to find funding elsewhere. When this happens, you may want or need to enter into another kind of business model:

2. Partnership – these are made up of two or more people and any profits, debts and decisions related to the **business** are a shared responsibility. Partnerships are common for practices that offer services such as accountants, dentists, doctors, solicitors and so on.

3. Company – the correct name for this is a joint stock company and it's made up of a number of people who put their money together to form a 'joint stock' of capital. These people are more commonly known as shareholders and, as the word suggests, they each own a share of the **business** and each expect a share of the profits too.

Each shareholder puts money into the company and receives a portion of the company – shares – equivalent to what they put in.

Despite each shareholder owning a piece of the company, in law it is seen as a legal entity – the same as an individual – that is entirely separate from the shareholders or members, as they are sometimes known. It can be sued, make a profit or loss, be held responsible for its employees' actions and go into liquidation – the term used for companies that go bankrupt.

4. Private Limited Companies – Most small businesses are private limited companies with the shares only available privately, for example, to family members. The shares are not available to buy publicly so they cannot be traded on the stock market.

5. Public Limited Companies – Being a Public Limited Company (PLC) is much more complex and is usually reserved for larger companies. To be called a PLC a company must have, amongst other things, more than one director and a trading certificate from Companies House. PLCs can sell their shares on the stock market, so anyone can buy them. Whilst it is easier to raise money using this method it also means that the company accounts are in the public domain. The company must also be audited and make certain information available to Companies House. Plus, PLCs can be bought out by other shareholders.

6. Franchises – A franchise involves you using another company's successful business model to create your own shop, restaurant etc. Essentially, you buy the franchise and trade off the good name of the company you've bought into. For example, Subway – you'd find a suitable location, Subway would provide you with their livery, food products and use of trademark. You make money because customers are already familiar with Subway; so you have an instant customer base. Franchises are for a fixed period of time – from five to 35 years – and cover a certain location known as a 'territory'. You'll have to pay the following:

1. fees to the franchisor
2. royalties for using the trademark
3. fees for the training and advice received

There are specific and complex laws relating to franchise contracts so entering into one is something that needs to be thought about very carefully.

7. Workers Co-operatives – This is a truly egalitarian form of business that is formed to meet the mutual needs of the workers. Each person – from the managing director to the shop floor assistant – is equally important. All decisions are taken democratically, and any profits are shared equally or ploughed back into the business. Co-operatives follow seven guiding principles:

1. Voluntary and open membership
2. Democratic control
3. Member economic participation (financial interest)
4. Autonomy and independence
5. Education, training and information
6. Co-operation among co-operatives
7. Concern for the community

This should give you a pretty good idea of the ethical and moral stance of a co-operative.

8. Limited Liability Partnerships (LLPs) – LLPs are a relatively new form of business as they've only been around since 2001. They are intended to benefit professional partnerships such as lawyers, accountants and the like, who are restricted from forming limited companies due to restrictions from their professional bodies. LLPs operate in much the same way as limited partnerships and allow the members to limit their personal liability if something goes wrong with the business.

So, as you can see, **businesses** can be simple or complex but, once you know what all the terminology means you should find it quite easy to decide which kind of **business** structure will best suit your needs.

Business training can help you start your own business.

The **three pillars must be diversified** and there are many ways to do this. From pensions, ISA's and bonds; to real estate and intellectual assets like books and song lyrics. Famous songs written by musicians that are no longer alive, are still making millions; it is a perfect example of where your passion and potential can be turned into profit and abundance by doing what you love.

Having an entrepreneurial mindset helps when it comes to creating wealth. If you venture out into the business world be sure to do your research and go for the business model that meets your aims, targets and desired outcomes.

Before You Invest: Due Diligence

After addressing the spiritual aspects of wealth increase, you must make sure that you do not neglect several natural details. Before you invest take steps to follow the principle of due diligence.

Due diligence is simply investigating potential investment before you invest. Whatever you fail to learn about investing may cost you money in the long run because ignorance is expensive. You must make sure you apply due diligence before investing.

Some of the steps you can take when applying due diligence may include consulting the **Financial Services Register**, run by the Financial Conduct Authority (FCA), to check the firm you decide to buy through is authorised to provide the types of investment or services that you're interested in. If a firm isn't authorised, report it to the FCA or police and do not do business with it.

Read the key facts or key investor information documents for the investment before you buy. These documents set out important information that the provider must tell you (these are not required for specific single/direct holdings of stocks and shares for example, not shares held in a fund or unit trust). If there is anything you do not understand, contact the provider for further details. If you're still unsure, you might want to consult a financial adviser.

Check what fees and charges you will have to pay. Charges for the same product might vary according to how you buy or which broker you choose. So, compare the cost of buying through different routes and firms.

Check the approach; be cautious of unsolicited approaches by phone call, text message, email or a person knocking on your door.

When applying due diligence, you must think about things like:

1. What can you afford to lose? Remember, when you invest – whatever capital you invest, view it as the *maximum you can lose but minimum you can gain!* This will help you decide what your risk level is.
2. What are the possible ways you could lose money with this investment?
3. Does the investment make good business sense?
4. Have you looked at the numbers? (Profit and margin trends, net income, revenue etc.)

5. What is your exit strategy?

Be sure to do your homework and understand the investment you are making. Below are some flags to look out for when checking if an investment or pension opportunity is a scam:

1. When a firm doesn't allow you to call it back.
2. Where you're forced to make a quick decision, or are pressured into doing so.
3. You are being offered a high return on your investment, but are told it is low risk.
4. Contact details you are given, or on their website, are only mobile phone numbers or a PO box address.

Risk And Returns

As mentioned earlier, there is nothing as no risk in any investment; there are low, medium and high-risk investments.

Risk is like faith, the more you stretch it is the more you grow it. You need to understand the level of risk for each asset before investing.

While assets with low risk are good as foundational bedrock investments, you will not earn passive income from them! Although it is essential to have them as insurance to safeguard your pyramid, you need to understand you will not earn income on these types of classes.

In contrast medium risk assets will give you income passively but you need to invest in them for longer terms.

High velocity will give you higher returns at short-term, but they are risky. This is the reason we will go on to discuss how to balance risk with the trickle exercise. The returns from high velocity assets need to be put into passive assets and your returns from passive assets need to be allocated to purchase more bedrock assets.

Apply The FRESH Principle To An Investment

After completing due diligence, you will need to apply the **Fresh Principle** before deciding to invest. Fresh, stands for:

Fixed or appreciating returns. Does the investment have fixed and appreciating returns especially when you invest in bonds, loan notes and any other risky investments?

Realistic returns. Returns must be able to cater for the four devils (tax, interest, inflation and exchange rate)

Exit strategy. This must be in place – establish whether the investment is short-term or long-term.

Secure investments on an asset to ensure your capital and returns are guaranteed.

Hands off as this is not a job it's a business and investment that should be growing without you needing to be directly involved/hands-on.

The Four Devils

A true investor will always need to consider three or four main areas before investment. I call these areas the four devils that can reduce or destroy the main benefit of your investment i.e. the returns. I describe the four devils fully in my book *Creating Wealth from Within*.

I describe the four devils as TIIE because whilst ties are decorative, they can be lethal – you can *'strangle' your rewards* if you fail to plan well and take due diligence as well as the necessary advice before investing:

1. **Tax** can affect investment returns if you don't have a good tax specialist to advise you on the best way to hold any investment where tax is applicable to you as an individual. There are various types of tax to consider (income capital, vat, inheritance tax etc).
2. **Inflation.** This erodes the value of investment which is the reason you must take account of it to make sure you look for realistic returns that pay well above inflation or are linked to inflation.
3. **Interest rates** – This is what is either paid on your savings, which is now at a record low, and if you are a borrower then any increase in rates of borrowing can reduce you returns.
4. **Exchange rates** – This is the rate you exchange your currency - especially if you invest overseas. It's crucial to consider what the currency rate is before investing as the returns may be reduced, if you need to exchange the returns back to your local currency.

Once you decide to invest, you must review your investment continually, employ and apply whatever strategies are applicable to changes in the market.

After you invest you must continue to keep up to date with your investment. It's like a farmer who plants seeds down in the ground, you must ensure you pull the weeds out from time to time otherwise there won't be a good harvest of fruit expected. Investment works in the same way – you can't just 'invest and go' or do nothing once the investment is made. Successful investment involves keeping an eye on your investment – as the market changes, your strategies may need to change too.

The most important action you must take when it comes to money that's been invested is what I call the three M's – they are essential practices required for your investments to grow:

1. Measure
2. Monitor
3. Manage

One of the best ways to review and manage your pillars is to apply a **trickle effect**, as shown in 'The Wealth Trickle Down' diagram. This is where you invest the extra returns you have on the high risk / velocity short-term investments back into the passive asset class, and in turn back to bedrock or foundation asset class. This will help to ensure your pyramid is growing and remains strong to withstand the changes in any market.

The Wealth Trickle Down

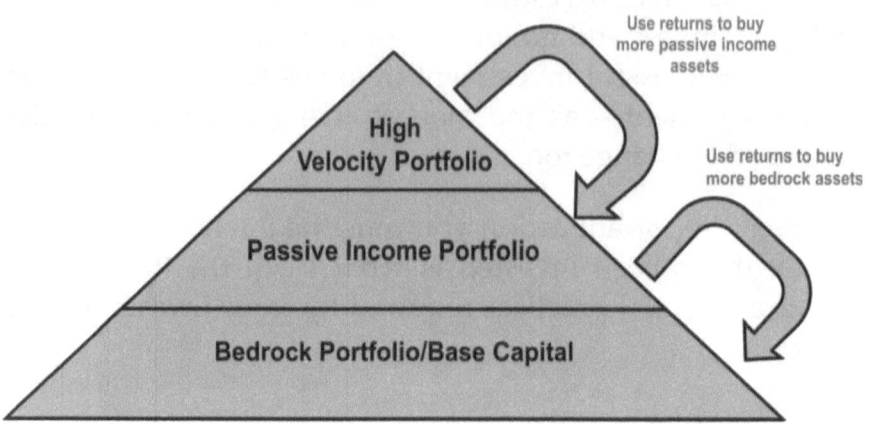

Wealth Protection: The felt and roof

To have a strong building or pyramid not only you must have strong pillars in place, you also need felt to line the roof as the base material before putting on the shingles – the felt acts as a backup waterproof membrane to protect against leakage. The same principle is required when you are building or creating wealth. So, let's take a closer look:

Felt Wealth Pyramid

Felt holds things together: you must have teams and systems in place when creating wealth because teams and systems are like the felt on a roof, they provide protection and hold things together.

Team: You must have the right team of specialists to deal with specialist areas that may affect your estate (accountants, tax specialists, contractors/builders, financial advisers' solicitors etc.).

Tax specialists will advise you in the area of various taxes including inheritance, estate, income, capital and various other taxes affecting business and investment. As mentioned above if you are in the property business, you will need contractors, builders, estate agents, letting agents, bankers, financial advisers etc.

System: *A system is a collection of elements or components that are organised for a common purpose. The word sometimes describes the organisation or plan itself. Just like a computer cannot function without its system – neither can a person who desires to create lasting wealth.*

<u>A computer system consists of hardware components that have been carefully chosen, so that they work well together, and software components or programs that run in the computer.</u>

To become a successful investor, you **must** have a great system and team in place. The right people, along with good systems, will make all of the difference to the survival and growth of your business and investment profitability.

Wealth Pyramid Roof Protection

Just like building a house requires a roof for protection from the elements, once you begin to build your investments you must ensure you protect them too. Your 'investment roof' includes having in place a WILL and **POWER OF ATTORNEY, as well as INHERITANCE AND ESTATE PLANNING.**

Without the roof to protect the building, external weather influences like rain, snow and sun may cause damage to the whole pyramid and cause it to crumble. The value will start to diminish.

Likewise to create lasting wealth and a financial legacy that can be passed on to the next generation – you must have a solid roof protection.

A **will** is a legal document that allows you to make clear what you want to happen to your estate once you are gone. **A will protects your assets and follows your written wishes for the benefit of your loved ones. Some even go further to draft a lifetime trust because** a will can only dispose of the assets that you own at the date of your death. If the value is eroded during your lifetime, there will be little, if anything, left for your beneficiaries to inherit – this is the reason for lifetime living trusts. They are specifically designed to protect your assets for you during your lifetime. They give you the peace of mind that your estate can be passed on securely and intact to your spouse, your children and their bloodline, or other named beneficiaries after your death.

Lasting power of attorney: A **power of attorney** protects your own interests while you're still alive – up to the point where you die. The moment you die, the power of attorney ceases and your will becomes relevant instead.

A lasting power of attorney (LPA) allows your loved ones to take care of you and your finances if you become unable to do so yourself.

There are two types of LPA:

A *'Property and Financial Affairs' LPA* gives your attorney the authority to deal with buying and selling your property, bills, bank accounts and investments.

A *'Health and Welfare' LPA* covers decisions about health and care and even decides where someone is to live. This can only be used if someone is incapable of dealing with such matters themselves. An LPA ensures that, should you be unable to manage your own affairs, the people you have appointed can manage your financial life on your behalf. This can save a great deal of money and distress, and will ensure that as a vulnerable person, your affairs will be handled correctly and quickly.

According to the Alzheimer's Society, more than 1 million people in the UK will have dementia by 2025. More than 1 in 5 people over 85 already suffer from it, with rates significantly higher amongst women than men. Accidents, strokes, brain injuries and Parkinson's disease can also affect someone's ability to make their own decisions. Handling your financial affairs can become virtually impossible, which is why charities who care for the elderly recommend everyone plans ahead; it could also have the dual benefit of saving a great deal of money and easing the burden on relatives.

If you lose mental capacity without an LPA in place, it will be necessary for your family to apply to the Court of Protection to have a deputy appointed to deal with everyday financial matters. This is a slow and very expensive process, costing thousands of pounds. If you must use a lawyer, it could cost a lot more. If you already have an LPA in place, this will not be necessary.

As you can see these are essential types of protection that are required if you are to pass wealth onto the next generation. The pyramid diagram shows what the **finished product should look like** after you have gone through each of the steps previously described throughout this chapter and the previous ones.

Systems and teams are towards the top of the pyramid because you need a good team and the right systems in place, as well as a strong foundation (which is your mindset) and secure pillars (RIB) to hold everything together:

Bottom tier: This is the foundation – your mindset is what everything else is built upon.

1st tier: Your pillars should be real estate, investments and business (RIB). The pillars will keep the structure upright and strong.

2nd tier: This is your teams and systems, felt holds things together. As discussed, you must have the right team of specialists to deal with specialist areas that may affect your estate (accountants, tax specialists, contractors/builders, financial advisers, solicitors etc.).

Top tier: The roof protects your pillars. It includes your will, tax protection, inheritance tax, estate planning and power of attorney.

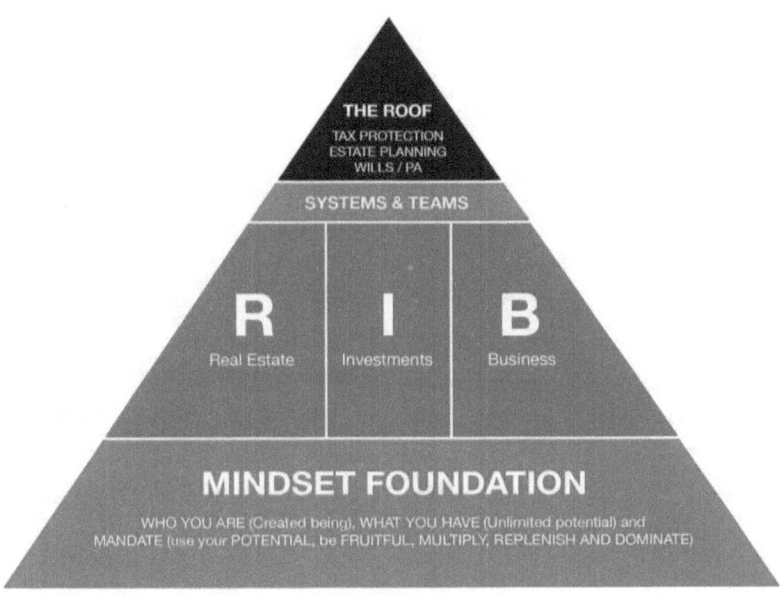

Summary diagram above

The roof of a solid pyramid ensures you have a will, a power of attorney and robust insurance in place to protect your estate.

By having a will you can leave clear instructions that provide the opportunity to order your affairs so everything is as you desire after your death.

A will helps reduce the amount of inheritance tax that might be payable on the value of the property and money you leave behind; this is especially important if you have children or other family who depend on you financially, or if you want to leave a legacy to people outside your immediate family.

Your final outcome is becoming a STAR INVESTOR!

How To Be A STAR Investor

Once you put all these principles in place and apply them, taking necessary steps of due diligence and learning to understand the financial world, your *ultimate goal is to be what I call a STAR investor who creates lasting wealth*. So, what does it mean been a STAR INVESTOR?

Success in investment doesn't just happen. There is a process and a path that can lead you to ensuring you become a star investor and make good solid investments that yield great returns!

So, exactly how do you become a star investor? Let's take a look at the four main areas you will need to focus on:

S – Strategy: Have a **flexible strategy** that works and is adaptable to changing market conditions. For example, real estate investment has several possible strategies depending on what you aim to achieve:

If you are looking for income then one or several of the following strategies will prove beneficial; BTL, HMO, rent to rent, service accommodation etc.

If you are trying to achieve capital growth then flipping real estate (buy low, sell high or buy something that you repair and fix before reselling at a profit) may work.

Strategy is important to the goals you set, when it comes to achieving them – you must be flexible and adopt the right strategies that help you.

<u>T – Team:</u> Have a robust **team** of professionals whom you are able to leverage on in terms of their professional specialities i.e. accountants, solicitors, tax specialists and managers. (Remember, if you are in the property business your team should also include contractors, plumbers, builders, architects, planners and estate and letting agents.) Your team is like felt holding your pillars together. People, systems and teams are paramount. Life was never designed for us to exist in isolation; remember, God made us to be *interdependent of each other*. It's safe to say that you don't know everything; in the Bible, James 1:5 says that if we lack wisdom, we should ask for it and God will give it to us liberally:

If any of you lack wisdom, let him ask of God, that giveth to all men liberally, and upbraided not; and it shall be given him. – James 1:5

<u>A – Attitude:</u> The **attitude** of an investor includes courage and imagination. There is no discouragement, no fear of temporary political or economic collapse or Brexit. Investors are dreamers and start with whatever comes to their hands, they are patient and have a no waste mentality; an investor is also focused, has a long-term view, is confident and able to take risks. There is no investment that is free of risk, but risk can be measured; you can have low, medium or high-risk investments.

<u>R –Returns:</u> The **returns** are what I call the fruit of your labour! You must always plan and prepare your investment and expect good rewards and returns on them! Business is different from charity. Charity begins when you have something to give. Don't invest in losing investments that

inflation and tax erode away daily! Others have to **see** your good works first! If there is no profit, then there is no investment or seed for reinvestment!

Now that we have dealt with some of the practical aspects, we will take a closer look at a few other areas that need to be addressed before you can begin your wealth creation journey.

Chapter Seven
THE WORD IN ACTION

I am the LORD thy God which teacheth thee to profit, which leadeth thee by the way that thou shouldest go.

– Isaiah 48:17

Problems Are Opportunities

You have a ***seed of potential*** *uniquely engineered* within your make up – you already have the ingredients around you! Yes, God gave **you** the ***ingredients*** *of opportunity and time* like everyone else. Time and opportunity are available to all, irrespective of your location. Whether you are from a first or third world country, whether rich or poor, no matter the difference in ethnicity, race or gender; we all have time and opportunity in common – we all have equal time allotted to us daily.

'Well', I hear you say, 'I don't have opportunities in my country.' Do you see problems? Do you have a solution to any of the problems you see around you no matter how insignificant they may be? If your answer is yes, then you have opportunity. You see, opportunity comes from the problems around you that your mind has a solution for. This is what will create your wealth. Let me ask you, what problems can you see around you right where you are? Is the solution of how to solve that problem flowing from your mind? Ideas, that were hidden before you began to see problems, will start to emerge and present opportunity for you!

You are a problem solver to someone else's problems. There is an opportunity for you to create abundance. That solution comes from the unique seed of greatness in you called potential. Your potential may be in the form of gifts, abilities etc.

Proverbs 18:16 says, 'A person's gift opens doors for him, bringing him access to important people.'[xvi] Your gift will make a way for you. Where others see a door as a barrier, you will see a door of opportunity open for you.

If you are in the UK, don't view Brexit as something negative. Instead, view it as an opportunity for those who can answer the problems Brexit creates.

There have been many lucrative deals made in the transport sector. The Department of Transport has had to secure additional capacity in light of a no-deal Brexit. This has led companies, who would otherwise have never had a chance, to profit. The government even awarded a £13.8m ferry freight contract to Seabourn Freight; a company that has no ships and no track record as a cross-Channel operator.[xvii]

This concept of opportunity works vice-versa. Foreign investors, including the Chinese, have swamped the UK to invest in real estate as the British pound lost its value against their currency. Real estate became cheaper for them and they took the opportunity. It is about how you choose to use the time and opportunity available to you that will determine your path from lack and debt to wealth.

How you use the opportunities open to you (i.e. the problems around you), how you use the experiences and training you have received and how you respond to external factors – including political and economic changes, as well as the problems associated with them, will determine how you can unlock your potential in creating wealth. You already have the seed to create wealth, i.e. your potential, you need to find the good soil of your mind and nurture the potential so that the fruit of greatness can emerge.

The Covenant[xviii]

From a biblical perspective, a covenant is a 'deal enacted by God, based on well-defined terms and sealed with an oath.'[xix] The entire Bible is a book of covenants and it is these covenants, or promises, that allow us to access every single thing we need for life.

If you desire to have **financial dominion, you must understand the covenant your Creator has made with you. God said,** 'My covenant will I not break, nor alter the thing that is gone out of my lips.' –Psalm 89:34 (KJV). **The words of man can and will fail, but God's word will not! His promises are yes and amen!**

To walk in financial dominion, you must first understand the God-given covenant that has made wealth available to you. If you truly want the covenant to work for you, then you must believe it, accept it and receive it. God's promises are not just for the people in the Bible, they apply to you today in the here and now.

The enemy does not want you to know the truth about finances because it will keep you from receiving! It's not about achieving; it's about believing in the One who made you and realising what you have within you.

So, exactly what is the covenant you have with God? When God created mankind, He blessed them and said:

Be fruitful: Meaning you have potential inside you, in the form of seed, to produce fruit.

Multiply: Multiplication is increase that supersedes

addition. It is not greed or unnecessary extravagance because multiplication is not just for you as you need to use it to bless the world!

Dominion: Abundance will give you dominion over everything. This is not a license to exercise control over others. Notice it is dominion over all things – meaning you don't have any excuse and can no longer say, 'I don't have any money or opportunities.' Take mastery over the things around you and exercise your authority. It does not matter where you come from – a first or second world country, nor does the colour of skin make a difference. You can take dominion over your environment and change your surroundings by exercising your God-given authority.

The covenant you have with God is an agreement that can never be changed. God first established it with Abram (later called Abraham) with His promise to make Abram the father of many nations. God gave him land and so much more as his inheritance. Abram was extremely wealthy! (Deuteronomy 28).

Abraham believed God and it was credited to him as righteousness (Genesis 15:6 and Romans 4:3). But there is so much hope because we see that Abraham did not do everything right. He lied and said that his wife was his sister and he got tired of waiting on God for his promised son and took another wife. In spite of all his mistakes, he was able to believe what God said about him and called himself the father of many nations.

It was Abraham's obedience and complete trust in God that resulted in his increase, wealth and fulfilled promises. All you need to do is believe in your Creator. He has given you the potential, power and authority to create wealth – you just need unlock it through faith in His word and make a quality decision to believe Him and obey Him – knowing that He will direct your path.

You may be thinking, *I know the covenant was meant for Abram, but was it really meant for me, too?*

In Galatians 3:13-14, we read that Christ died to redeem us from the curse of the law, 'that the blessing of Abraham might come on the Gentiles through Jesus Christ; that we might receive the promise...'*(KJV,* emphasis added). God sealed His covenant with you through the blood of Jesus, which means that agreement is **binding** and **forever**.

So, is the covenant reliable? God's word is true and because it is true **every covenant of Scripture is reliable, dependable, guaranteed and binding on God for delivery.** However, there is a clause. God is only ever obligated to deliver if you are able to uphold your end of the agreement by keeping His commandments (1 John 5:3). This means you must love God with all your heart, mind and soul (Matthew 22:37).

Are you ready to take back the financial dominion that belongs to you? If you can learn to resist the enemy and obey God's word concerning finances, then you will be able to **take financial dominion**.

This book has mapped out the principles I believe will help

you reclaim your dominion and authority and unlock the hidden wealth in your life.

Honour The Tithe

This world is governed by the law of seed, time and harvest. Both tithing and giving are financial principles that people often overlook. Do you want to receive? Then you must first learn how to tithe and give:

'Honour the Lord with your possessions, and with the first fruits of all your increase; <u>so your barns will be filled with plenty, and your vats will overflow with new wine.</u>*' –Proverbs 3:9-10, NKJV (emphasis added)*

I am sure that you are aware of the adage 'you reap what you sow.' If you desire for God to honour you and bless you in the area of your finances, then you are going to have to honour Him in the area of your finances. This means that you need to honour Him with your money. Proverbs 3:9 says you are to honour God, 'with the first fruits of all your increase.' Put plainly, this simply means that you need to tithe. The word *tithe* means 'tenth,' which is an instruction to give 10% of your gross income to the Lord.

Look at Malachi 3:10-11:

[10] Bring ye all the tithes into the storehouse, that there may be meat in mine house, and prove me now herewith, saith the LORD of hosts, if I will not open you the windows of heaven, and pour you out a blessing, that there shall not be room enough to receive it.

[11] And I will rebuke the devourer for your sakes, and he

shall not destroy the fruits of your ground; neither shall your vine cast her fruit before the time in the field, saith the LORD of hosts.

The above verses show how crucial tithing is to your finances. That's why the enemy has done such a good job in deceiving people about the tithe; he does not want you to walk in financial abundance which rightfully belongs to you. Do not step into the trap of the enemy and tell yourself that you can't afford to tithe because the truth is, you can't afford not to!

Bishop Oyedepo put it this way, 'Any believer who is not a tither will remain a financial struggler.' In fact, you will find that **all testimonies of financial blessing in the Body of Christ begin with consistent tithing.**

Biblical Giving

You must understand that **tithing and giving are different.** Giving is an offering that goes beyond the tithe, you cannot truly give without first tithing. Tithers are always generous givers because they go above and beyond the 10% previously discussed.

Biblical giving can be in the form of money, clothing, food or almost anything else God leads you to give. Have you noticed most organisations that are prospering regularly give to the homeless, run food banks, provide shelter and so on? Whether intentionally or not, they have accessed the principle of increase through their giving!

Giving is the way you increase in the kingdom of God, this

is because when you give, you are sowing seed for a harvest. You have a covenant of financial prosperity and dominion with God; meaning you should be overcoming all financial challenges and economic circumstances – you should have dominion over them!

Your giving will open the door to wealth creation. It will enable you to step through open doors of opportunity and continuously walk in financial dominion. If you want to increase more – learn to give more.

A few years ago, I wanted to break the barrier of just being a BTL (buy to let) landlord and diversify into DEVELOPMENT – this would require more money and more expertise! So, I started digging again by **asking questions**. With the leading of the Holy Spirit, I started looking at **what I had in my house first**, just like the widow in the Bible!

We are told in 2 Kings 4 that the widow was faced with a dire financial need. She owed money to a creditor and cried out to a prophet for help, she did not want to lose her sons and have them sold into slavery to pay the debt. The prophet told her to bring what she had in her house, a small jar of olive oil. God used the very thing she had to take her out of debt and into abundance.

As I looked at what I had, money came to me in a number of ways; loans that I had given out were restored and I was repaid, and some assets, of which I didn't know their worth, were revealed to me by my broker! Before I knew it, I was able to put together £2.5M.

The next stage was deciding which assets to invest in. I didn't have a contact so I started digging again and someone who I never imagined could pass me a property deal, as it's not his profession, called me and told me about a school and a restaurant that had just been shut down; the owner wanted a private sale. I jumped with joy and purchased both assets in cash.

These events did not take place by chance, my habit of giving – FOLLOWING THE DIRECTION OF the Holy Spirit – helped me obtain the assets at a good price. I recall being led to give £5k while waiting for the owner to reduce one of the assets from £1m to £975k, which the owner had refused to accept three times already. Suddenly, the owner contacted us back and asked me to take the assets for £925k! That was a saving of ten-times my £5k giving!

Defeating The Enemy

The book of James 4:7 says, 'Submit yourselves therefore to God. Resist the devil, and he will flee from you'. So, _how can you resist the devil? The answer is right under your nose. You resist the devil with the words that you speak, so you must watch what you say! Develop a tenacious and determined kind of faith and continue to speak words of life by always keeping the word of God in your eyes, ears and mouth._

If you are **in debt**, you must take the necessary steps to get out by taking action. As long as you are in debt you will be a slave to your finances. Please note, when referring to debt, I do not include debt for investments that will grow in value or generate long-term income.

Financial Provision

Financial provision comes from the Lord. It is God that *gives you the ability, the power and the know-how to create and build wealth.*

Deuteronomy 8:18 (NIV): But remember the LORD your God, for it is He who gives you the ability to produce wealth, and so confirms His covenant, which He swore to your ancestors, as it is today.

Like any parent, God has a genuine desire to meet your needs. But He wants to go beyond that by giving you of His riches and furnishing you in abundance!

Philippians 4:19 (NLT): And this same God who takes care of me will *supply all your needs* from His glorious riches, which have been given to us in Christ Jesus.

Proverbs 10:22 (NLT): The *blessing of the Lord makes a person rich, and He adds no sorrow with it.*

2 Corinthians 9:8 (NLT): And God will generously provide all you need. Then you will always have everything you need, and plenty left over to share with others.

Jeremiah 17:7-8 (NLT, emphasis and italics added): But blessed are those who trust in the Lord and have made the Lord their hope and confidence. They are like trees planted along a riverbank, with roots that reach deep into the water. Such trees are not bothered by the heat or worried by long months of drought. *Their leaves stay green, and they never stop producing fruit.*

Whether there is Brexit or not, irrespective of who is in authority in your nation; it doesn't matter if the market is up or down or even if there is famine – you will experience and walk in the blessing if you put your trust in the Lord.

God does not do anything without the following three things:

1. *Faith*
2. *Love*
3. *Seed*

Faith: *It is impossible to please God without it. (Hebrews 11:6)*

Love: *The greatest commandment we have been given is love – you are to love your neighbours as yourself. (Mark 12:28-29)*

Seed: *Without seed God cannot do anything. God is obligated to multiply the seed that you give back to Him. John 3:16 tells us God so loved the world that* He gave.

Believing without taking action is fruitless.

Take Financial Dominion

If you have done or are currently doing the things I have mentioned in this chapter then there is only one thing left to do. You must continue to stand in faith until you see the promises of God fulfilled.

Ephesians 6:13 (ESV) puts it this way, 'Therefore take up the whole armour of God, that you may be able to withstand in the evil day, and having done all, to stand firm.'

You must stand! Do not draw back, cave in, give up or quit. Continue to stand on God's promises and know that the covenant of financial dominion is for you!

When speaking of patience, W.E. Vine said, 'Patience is the quality that does not surrender to circumstances or succumb under trial: it is the opposite of despondency and is associated with hope.'

Don't neglect the **power of patience**, because you need patience to receive the promise of financial dominion! (Hebrews 10:36). Don't be greedy and don't despise small beginnings. Being jealous and envious of those who have made their gains and attempting to copy them is really unwise because you do not know how they arrived where they are. Some have made their money by robbing innocent people! God promises to bless the work of your hands – trust Him!

Remember, God's covenant has never failed, and it will not fail you. But you must do your part and walk out the covenant through obedience, faith and patience. Then, **every financial stress will be terminated in Jesus' Name.**

Hidden Wealth

CONCLUSION

"For as he thinks in his heart, so is he"
- Proverbs 23:7

"The will to win is not nearly as important as the will to prepare to win. Everyone wants to win but not everyone wants to prepare to win."
- Bobby Knight

Thinking

We've all heard people say you are what you eat; but there is a much more important saying everyone should pay attention to: You are what you repeatedly think.

What you think, determines what you do and what you repeatedly do determines who you are or who you become. The mind, and all that goes on within it, is a perfect representation of what you are as well as who you are. Consistently think negative thoughts and you will become a negative person that produces negative results.

If what you think is so vital to who you are and where you are then you must take time to think about what you're thinking about.

How does a thought begin? For some it begins as an image, or something that has been read, which triggers a thought or starts the thought process.

If I said the words 'big dog' – what would you think of? Do you think of the words and letters or do you start to picture the image of a big dog?

Our thoughts always form images which are linked to emotions and feelings. Thoughts are often triggered by our five senses; what we see, feel, taste, touch, smell or hear. That's why you can smell a scent and be transported back to a special moment in your past.

Remember, changing your actions alone is never enough. We see this time and time again within the arena of weight loss. A person desires to lose weight so they change their diet and spend time exercising; all external factors. Do they lose weight? Yes – of course they do! However, they very rarely keep the weight off. Why? Because they have only dealt with the external. They have failed to address the real issues, which are internal, and eventually their old habits of eating and lack of exercise creep back into their daily routine.

Those that lose weight and keep it off are usually the ones who also work on the internal. They have looked at why their diets were bad, why they overate or why they couldn't exercise consistently. They then changed their 'why' by changing the way they thought about food, diet and health.

To change any area of your life, you must first change the way you use your mind. Every single successful person has done this, whether consciously or otherwise. Our minds are creatures of habit and we can train them to be successful or continue to fail and yield the same old mediocre results.

In Jesus' time, the Sadducees only believed in what they could observe with their five senses. If they could not see, feel, taste, touch or hear it then it wasn't real[xx].

The Bible teaches us that we are spirit, soul and body and that the three are, to an extent, separate, but integrated entities[xxi]. Each of us is a spirit, we each have a soul (your mind, will and emotions) and we each live in a physical body. The mind is composed of three main areas which are intellect, emotions and free will.

Negative thoughts are toxic thoughts. If a person's mind is empowered by positive thoughts, then they can make good choices that will positively change their physical body and shape the world around them.

Wealth is not an IQ game, it's a mind game. The fruits of your thoughts are ideas that can create wealth so if you get your mind right, you can 'win the game.'

Until a mixture of concrete is set, you cannot have a solid structure. If you think on something frequently enough, it sets like a mixture of concrete. That is why right mind renewal is the only way you can build successfully.

Set minds stand firm on their beliefs and once they are set, they can be very difficult to move. I have learnt that, 'The best skill set without the right mindset will eventually leave you upset.'

It is impossible to create wealth or achieve true success without first aligning the way you think. Successful people don't just do successful things, they think like successful people think. But what exactly does it mean to think successfully?

What you think has an impact on every single part of your life. Wealth creators think many of the following thoughts daily:

1. I make no excuses
2. Nothing is impossible
3. I follow through
4. It takes me what it takes
5. I master the details
6. I learn from failures

7. I focus on what matters
8. I collaborate and/work with others
9. I make my decisions
10. I develop my thoughts

Imagination

'Imagination will often carry us to worlds that never were. But without it we go nowhere.' – Carl Sagan

Imagination is a beautiful thing. Most of what we enjoy today is as a result of the creativity and resourcefulness that has taken place in the mind of an individual. When you imagine, you form new ideas and concepts; you see with the 'mind's eye'.

I am fully persuaded that if a person can learn to change and align the way they think – then their progress, success and ability to create wealth will follow suit.

Most people in the western world have enough money to make money; they just don't see the potential around them – this is due to wrong thinking and a lack of creativity.

Your imagination is the best way to tap into the potential that you have because your mind is the door that can unlock your wealth creation possibilities.

Mankind was given imagination to achieve the impossible. If you can see a problem, then a solution is also available – you just need to locate it. Solutions begin within your mind and are dependent upon how you choose to think about the problems presented to you.

Five Levels Of Wealth Creation

Wherever you start from either financial insecurity or financial security, the steps here will help you to track where you are and where you ought to be. For a reminder, view the diagram below again.

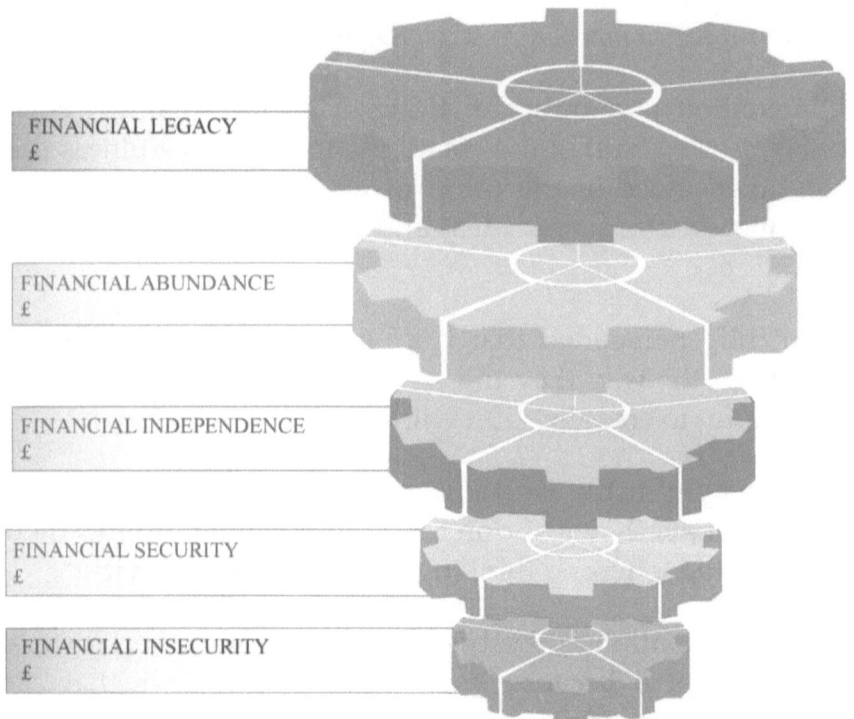

The diagram above, as seen in chapter 5, gives a clear picture of what the levels of wealth creation should look like:

You go from **financial insecurity** (more month than money and never being able to make ends meet) to **financial security** (bills = income). The next level is **financial independence** (which is passive income = expenses PILE). From **financial independence** you are able to step into <u>**financial abundance**</u>, this is where you can meet the needs of others. Once you have reached this level you can move to the final stage which is <u>**financial legacy**</u>. This stage is where you are not only able to meet the needs of others, but where you leave a legacy for the generations to come. Financial legacy is where your wealth is able to go beyond the here and now and transcend your lifespan. It is where your wealth can still make a difference even after you have left this earth.

<u>Testimonials</u>

Testimonies are powerful, it says in the Bible that they overcame by the blood of the lamb and the word of their testimony (Revelation 12:11).

I have often found that hearing about the stories of others helped me along my wealth creation journey and aided in achieving my goals. Below, are some testimonials from people I have mentored. Read them and be encouraged – they have been able to unlock the wealth that lies within and so can you!

"Mentorship has helped me gain understanding in many different aspects, when dealing with investment and all areas of life in general. After receiving mentorship from Elizabeth, I have learned valuable lessons that have proved priceless:

1. Working a 12-hour shift in exchange of my time for money has a limit.
2. My income is not wealth.
3. The need to change my mindset and invest in assets that will outlast my generation.
4. What to look out for in an investment; the principles.
5. Be flexible when managing situations.
6. Always have a positive attitude and respond positively.
7. Never panic but work to find a way out because a good solution is always out there to find!"
   - Toyin, NHS Manager

"I have gained significant insight on investments in property and other areas, like commodities, that are high in value and returns. I am now motivated to start doing other things because of the way I have been encouraged. Elizabeth's mentorship has given me direction on how to go into multiple streams of income (diversification), thinking ahead and having a retirement plan.

I have benefited in learning about having a good understanding on the importance of the mind, reasons to have a business and managing my time effectively: I can't increase TIME, but I can increase my finances!

As a result of the mentorship I have assessed my spending habits with a view to establishing the mindset of investing. I have looked at short and medium-term investments and I am still looking at other strategies for wealth creation through property investment and passive income like bonds, shares etc.

The ALIE Principle was the most important principle introduced to me! It was difficult for me to complete the assignment that came with the principle because I didn't want to face reality but, it now happens to be one of my most favourite principles because of the many benefits. Also, the ESSA Principle is a good foundation upon which I continue to reflect daily.

I am educating my household about wealth creation and delayed gratification. I am making every effort to apply these principles daily. By reducing my spending, cutting down on my liabilities, monthly, and looking at how to increase my income. Also, I have been confessing what my net worth will be by the time I retire, what I want to live on after retirement and what I want to leave for my children and their children."

- *Bosa, Local Authority Manager*

"Quite simply, Elizabeth's mentorship has changed my life. Her style of mentoring, her knowledge and expertise in her field and her determination to help you succeed are just inspiring. She helped me make sense of the financial chaos that I was in before I met her, she taught me financial discipline, how to focus on my goals and not waver from them even when faced with economic uncertainties.

The most important mantra that this amazing teacher, mentor and friend has taught me is to be 'debt free' – k for only then can you truly claim to be financially independent. I have had some amazing investment successes to date. I am very lucky to know Elizabeth as a friend because she has been incredible in holding my hand and guiding me through this exciting and sometimes challenging wealth journey."

- Teresa Company Director and Project Consultant

"What I have gained from the mentorship:

1. *A change in my mindset: A transformed MINDSET develops confidence, overcomes doubt and fear, shapes the attitude and develops greater capacity for success.*
2. *~~IM~~POSSIBLE (is a word in the dictionary): Initially, the thought of wealth creation was so daunting and I believed that I had to be a genius to succeed.*

The most important principles I have been taught:

1. *We all have been given time and opportunity, money is not the main tool for starting a business and creating wealth.*
2. *Everything starts from a seed, there is a seed inside of each one of us and if sown in the right soil, at the right time it will produce continually.*
3. *My talent/seed is not just for me alone but an opportunity to reach out and demonstrate love to those around me.*

How I practically implement the principles:

1. *Through regular monitoring, I am taking steps towards financial freedom by reducing my liabilities and increasing my assets – step by step.*
2. *Investing in low to medium risk investments by moving monies from low interest accounts to higher*

yielding projects.
3. *Because of my MINDSET change, the strength of my WHY is determining my daily routine, hence success is inevitable."*
   - *Betti Care Manager*

"It has been a world of experiences since joining mentorship with Elizabeth, I have come to understand that success is using what you have as a wise farmer to achieve what is needful. Elizabeth is selfless with information and has helped in walking me through the various processes and introducing me to other areas I have been overlooking or not had a full understanding of. I have been able to structure my assets and liabilities. I have been able to spread my savings into various investments like properties and ISA's, and taken advantage of what is out there financially.

For me, the most important principle is the principle of the SEED. The seed is in every experience and whatever passion I have.

I have purchased properties etc. as stated earlier. I am now using the leverage of others to achieve my aims. I have formed various teams for the various asset groups I have. I am on the verge of paying off the mortgage in the house I live in. I have opened various ledgers and have reviewed my assets and property leases. I have diversified my business and have other things in the pipeline.

I recommend Elizabeth's mentorship to anyone who wants to structure their life and wealth."

Hidden Wealth

- *Florence Company Director*

All human beings have been engineered with creative abilities, but they are hidden inside. To unlock them, you need to believe in the One who made you, understand your mandate, then realise and release your potential.

You already have the needed resources to create. If a farmer gave you an apple seed and some instructions but you fail to produce apples, i.e. the fruit, it either means you don't have a good relationship with the farmer or you didn't follow the instructions.

You have potential that is unique to you, and opportunities that surround you – yield to them and unlock your hidden wealth.

[i] http://mentalfloss.com/article/85007/how-michael-jackson-bought-publishing-rights-beatles-catalogue
[ii] https://en.wikipedia.org/wiki/KFC#cite_note-autogenerated52-13
[iii] https://en.wikipedia.org/wiki/KFC#cite_note-autogenerated44-6
[iv] https://en.wikipedia.org/wiki/KFC#cite_note-Binney2012-14
[v] https://en.wikipedia.org/wiki/KFC#cite_note-history-15
[vi] Neural Plasticity Volume 2014 (2014), Article ID 541870, 10 pages. Adult Neuroplasticity: More Than 40 Years of Research. Eberhard Fuchs and Gabriele Flügge.
[vii] Romans 12: 2 (NLT)
[viii] https://www.forbes.com/sites/forbesagencycouncil/2017/08/25/finding-brand-success-in-the-digital-world/
[ix] Daniel 1:20
[x] Bloomberg
[xi] Bankrate
[xii] https://en.wikipedia.org/wiki/Smoking_cessation
[xiii] https://themysteriousworld.com/top-10-largest-fast-food-chains-in-the-world/
[xiv] record.com/celebs
[xv] https://en.wikipedia.org/wiki/Liability_(financial_accounting)#cite_note-1
[xvi] Proverbs 18:16 ISV translation
[xvii] https://www.theguardian.com/politics/2018/dec/31/no-deal-brexit-ferries-who-gets-funds-and-how-was-contract-awarded
[xviii] https://blog.kcm.org/5-steps-take-financial-dominion/
[xix] Bishop David Oyedepo
[xx] Matthew 22:23-31, Acts 23:8
[xxi] Genesis 2:7, Matthew 26:41, 1 Thessalonians 5:23, Hebrews 4:12

www.ingramcontent.com/pod-product-compliance
Lightning Source LLC
Chambersburg PA
CBHW020918180526
45163CB00007B/2792